KIDGER

Inside Music

A Music Education Programme for Class Teaching (Preschool to Age 13)

First Steps: Age 7-11

Andrew Maddocks

the voices foundation
transforming children through singing

Published by The Voices Foundation and Alfred Publishing Co

"It is only when we get 'inside' music that we become fully aware of the skills and concepts involved in music education, and are able to come to terms with the cognitive functions of music and can appreciate the reasons behind music's great beauty. Above all, through individual musicianship development, music can take a key position in the way we live our lives and can help us to recognise that there is something beyond ourselves."

Michael Stocks

Inside Music is a music education programme pioneered and devised by Michael Stocks, a much respected person in the world of music education, an adviser in English state education for many years and a founding member with the Principal, Suzi Digby, of The Voices Foundation. **Inside Music** has been built upon Michael's many years of teaching experience, classroom research, careful and widespread observation of school music lessons and innumerable discussions with practising teachers. From his work and leadership and from the collective experience and advice of The Voices Foundation team of Advisory Teachers and Consultants, **Inside Music** provides a much-needed progression of learning over a wide age-range from birth to 13, ensuring continuity in the classroom from Year 1 to Year 9 and setting appropriate levels of teacher expectation for each stage according to pupil age and experience.

To enable initial access to this programme for teachers and early years practitioners the following handbooks have been produced:

■ *Early Years: To Age 5* by Beth Hill

Written by Beth Hill, this handbook provides a range of opportunities to help babies and under-5s to become comfortable with music activity, and to begin to experience some of the music basics by planting seeds for healthy growth in skills and knowledge in music education.

Published by The Voices Foundation and Alfred Publishing Co
© The Voices Foundation 2014

■ *First Steps: Age 5-7* by Andrew Maddocks

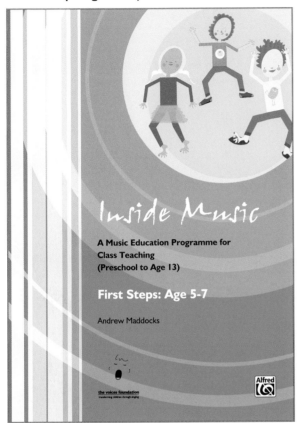

■ *First Steps: Age 7-11* by Andrew Maddocks

This handbook is based upon a careful selection of song material from which basic music skills and concepts are derived, including the use of percussion instruments and listening material.

This handbook provides an initial two-year programme for classes who are later newcomers to the **Inside Music** education approach. It provides song, recorded music and instrumental material from which aural, singing and playing skills are developed and from which concepts are derived to build the foundations of musicianship. It also prepares a pathway to the later stages of **Inside Music**.

Inside Music Online offers further support for teachers using the **First Steps** handbooks. Primary school subscribers are able to access additional resources, video footage of 'good practice' and regular upgrades as further developments take place.

Inside Music Online plans to provide a carefully structured baseline programme for Years 7 and 8 [ages 11–13] with a clear progression of learning and continuity through to Year 9. It will include a rich compilation of pedagogical suggestions, appropriate music repertoire and recommendations to assist the teacher in the creation of secondary school music schemes of work.

Published by The Voices Foundation and Alfred Publishing Co
© The Voices Foundation 2014

Acknowledgements

The Headley Trust

The Voices Foundation is extremely grateful to The Headley Trust for its financial generosity that has made this publication possible.

Michael Stocks

Our deepest gratitude goes to Michael Stocks, the creator of The Voices Foundation's methodology, who, over recent years, has created our new resource - **Inside Music** - from which **First Steps: Age 7-11** has been drawn.

We are grateful to our colleagues below for their advice and support in creating **First Steps: Age 7-11**

Consultative Group

Sally Cathcart
Rosemary Jones
Carole Kendall
Katie Neilson
Michael Stocks
Nicola Wallis

CD Singers

Ann Hains
Beth Hill
Jan Trott
Frances Webb

CD Co-ordinator

Caroline Sindall

Designer

Tracy Miles, Somerton Computing

We have made every effort to trace and acknowledge copyright owners. If any of them are not listed below, we offer our apologies and ask that you contact us immediately.

I, I, me oh my from Be a Real Musician - Geoffrey Russell-Smith
© Boosey & Hawkes Music Publishers Ltd 1977

Naxos Licensing

National Youth Choir of Scotland

Published by The Voices Foundation and Alfred Publishing Co
© The Voices Foundation 2014

Contents

Published by The Voices Foundation and Alfred Publishing Co
© The Voices Foundation 2014

First Steps: Age 7-11 is a handbook for KS2 teachers who teach pupils in Years 3 and upward. It forms part of the *Inside Music* programme and is primarily for children starting this particular education approach in Years 3 and 4. It can also be successfully used with starters in Years 5 and 6. The intention of this handbook is to provide an initial two-year practical guide to teaching. The aim is to establish confidence in both teacher and children, and to secure a progression of teaching and learning.

Central to the teaching process is performing, the act of making music. Performing gives the child the essential tactile experience of being '*Inside Music*'. At the very heart of the performing strand in this programme, singing provides the collective and personal experiences that can lead to shared enjoyment.

Performing also includes body action and movement and the playing of instruments. To an extent the two are related, the instrument being an extension of the body. The approach to an instrument ought to have regard for those things that will enable a progression of skills and make new things possible. In *First Steps*, when playing pitch [tuned] percussion, several basic beater techniques are introduced.

Performing in *First Steps* will introduce children to the early stages of singing with two voice parts, the early stages to singing chorally in the classroom and beyond.

By KS2 it is hoped that children will have already discovered their Singing Voice and will have some level of confidence in using it. However, *First Steps* will help those who still need to acquire their ability to match the pitch of others and to build on limited sureness. *First Steps* will also go much further and give children an insight into important aspects of singing development. Hence, they will learn about posture, breathing, singing in tune, tone quality, clarity and expressing the mood and lyrics of songs.

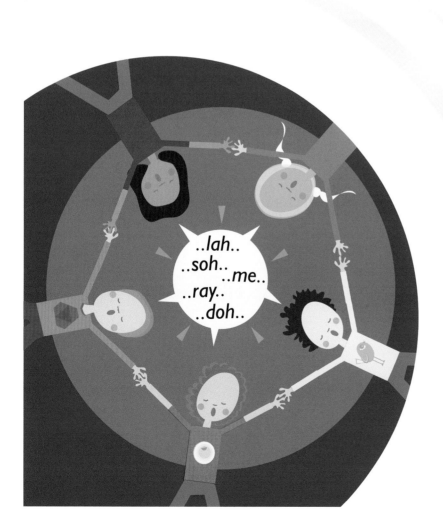

Listening and thinking are at the centre of all musical activity. There are several branches: listening to imitate; inner listening with the Thinking Voice to recall, identify and create; listening to others as they perform [listening in audience]; listening to recordings; and viewing and listening to videos. There are the finer skills of discrimination, eg distinguishing between one sound and another, or making decisions about how a song is to be sung. In *First Steps*, listening to recorded music, improvising, working with sol-fa and specific pitch intervals, instrument playing and part-singing enhance these listening skills.

The progressive understanding of concepts – pitch, rhythm [duration], structure, timbre, tempo, metre, dynamics and texture [what the National Curriculum 2014 calls 'inter-related dimensions'] – follows in the wake of the practical activities of performing, listening and thinking. In particular, by learning and using the songs assigned to each Unit, the children aurally absorb the musical information that each contains and which is directly relevant to the Teaching Objectives of the Unit. Thus, the teaching is drawing on actual first-hand and appropriate music experience.

First Steps offers structure, progression, teaching ideas, songs, listening material and guidance. It seeks to offer a teaching product of quality and substance, one that will realise the true musical potential of children. The book and CDs have been compiled with the intention of being as user-friendly as possible.

First Steps is a two-dimensional tool for a three-dimensional activity. Only the practitioner or the teacher can take the songs and teaching ideas off the page and bring them to life for the children. We believe there is no substitute for the personal and 'live' interaction between you and the children. Of course, there can be professional support from colleagues, and please bear in mind that The Voices Foundation offers complementary training.

Andrew Maddocks

Editor, *First Steps: Age 7-11*
Senior Adviser, The Voices Foundation

Published by The Voices Foundation and Alfred Publishing Co
© The Voices Foundation 2014

Published by The Voices Foundation and Alfred Publishing Co

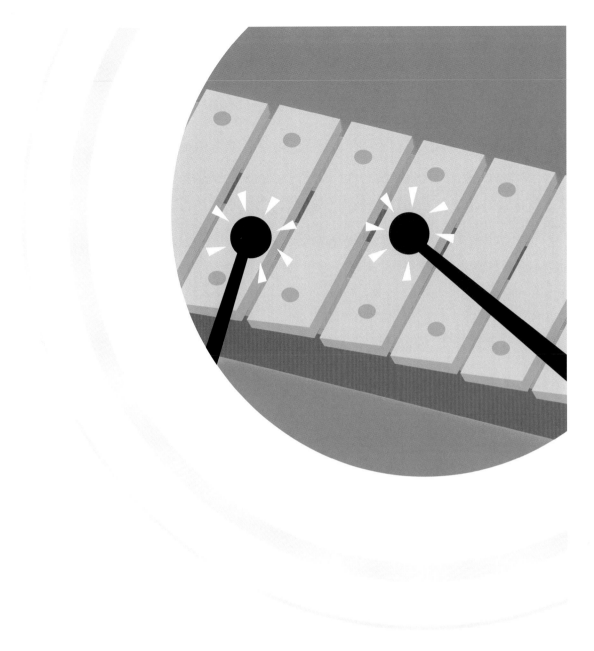

Planning For Music

Published by The Voices Foundation and Alfred Publishing Co
© The Voices Foundation 2014

What will *First Steps* provide for you and the children?

The Central Teaching and Learning Strands

- Singing skills
- Pitch [tuned] percussion playing skills
- Musicianship: a progressive development of skills and concepts

The Pathways for Teaching and Learning

- The songs
- The listening and thinking
- The practical and experiential activities

The Core Outcomes

- Improved singing abilities and sound quality
- The early stages of choral singing: performing with two voice parts
- Basic performing skills on pitch percussion instruments
- Developed aural, improvising and composing skills involving the Thinking Voice
- Developed knowledge of the concepts of pitch and rhythm, and the structural and expressive elements of phrase, tempo, metre, timbre, dynamics and texture [National Curriculum 2014: inter-related dimensions]
- Developed notational skills in reading and writing including the use of rhythm sol-fa

What will you do this term?

- The 22 **Teaching Units** and 2 **Revision Units** provide the platform for 6 terms of teaching
- Each **Unit** is the basis for several weeks of music teaching
- A **Unit** is <u>not</u> a single lesson plan!
- As a guide, you could aim to allocate three or four of the **Units** to each term

How will you allocate time for your teaching?

- Music performing and listening is a **transient experience**; it exists in time – it starts, it travels, it finishes – and is then only a **memory**
- This makes music learning very **memory-dependent**
- The **memory** is wonderfully agile and capable, but with the passing of **time**, **skills** and **knowledge** will fade, especially if they are relatively new and infrequently practised
- **Skills** require **regular practice** if a state of **habit-memory** [instant memory recall] is to be achieved
- **Music skills** are **aural memory** dependent, but are helped and prompted by associated **muscle memory** and **visual cues** and **symbols** [eg notation].
- **A STRATEGY OF 'LITTLE-AND-OFTEN' IS MUCH THE BEST FOR THIS TEACHING STAGE OF THE** *Inside Music* **PROGRAMME.**
- **LET'S AIM FOR A PLANNED 15 MINUTES EACH DAY – MINI-LESSONS!**

Published by The Voices Foundation and Alfred Publishing Co
© The Voices Foundation 2014

How do I get the best out of a Unit?

There are **three teaching phases**:

1. **Preparation**: new songs are learned and others revised

2. **Making Conscious**: teaching the skill or concept

3. **Practice**: reinforcing the new or continuing skills and understanding; assessing and deciding when to move on

During the **Preparation** phase, children acquire vital music experience for phase 2 through an in-depth assimilation of the teaching **Songs**.

During the **Making Conscious** phase, children become actively aware of the Unit's skill or concept focus through the songs and **Teaching Ideas**.

During the **Practice** phase, children are helped to acquire greater skill and understanding; if appropriate, they revisit on-going skills and concepts in preparation for the next Unit.

In reality, the **three phases** will usually overlap each other.

What does each Unit provide?

■ **Unit**

Each Unit is numbered and has a suggestion as to how long the teacher can expect to spend on each, assuming a 15-minute daily mini-lesson. However, it is only a guide, and the teacher should not feel confined by this.

■ **Focus**

There will always be two or more recurring strands.

■ **Teaching Objectives**

These are the skills and concepts to be taught.

■ **What is going to happen?**

These will summarise the teaching activities.

■ **Songs**

These are the song titles central to the teaching, songs to be used as part of the Singing Development and Hot Songs, which provide opportunities for sociable fun and activities. All songs are recorded on CD-1. It is not always necessary to learn all the listed songs. Some are alternatives or optional. Be guided by the requirements of the Teaching Activities.

*Important: Titles shown in italics are songs being used for the first time in **First Steps**. They will need to be taught and assimilated by the children before being used with the Teaching Ideas.*

Teachers with older pupils may wish to exercise their discretion whether to use songs annotated with an asterisk.

■ Listening

The listening examples are to be found on CD-2. All are directly or indirectly related to the Teaching Objectives of the Units; some have specific activities in Teaching Ideas. In addition, there are suggestions for video viewing on YouTube. These are relevant to the teaching, but, of course, their future availability cannot be guaranteed. Often the Listening tracks on CD-2 will have a visual equivalent on YouTube. Some videos have poor vision and sound quality. Others, not so, and provide the children with important visual information. It is suggested that searches can be rewarding and revealing.

■ General Guidance

This provides important observations about the teaching of the Unit.

■ Teaching Ideas

The teaching activities are grouped into sets, each with a heading. You will probably find some teaching ideas easier to teach than others. This is quite natural. Many of the sets have several teaching ideas that reinforce the same point of learning. You may be able to accomplish the teaching objective using an activity with which you feel more comfortable and set aside another. Do use your own judgement.

■ Learning Outcomes

The statements give the teacher hoped-for outcomes that should be observable and form the basis of an assessment.

What could a teaching plan for a Unit look like?

■ A Unit planning template can be found on page 13. This template can be found on CD-2.

■ There follow two completed exemplars.

■ Each Unit has sets of teaching activities. Plan these into each week.

■ Since repetition is an important part of the teaching process, the children benefit from the same or similar activities being used for several consecutive days.

■ For the development of skills involving the aural memory, the Thinking Voice and performing, eg singing development, the frequency of contact with those teaching activities is vital for the children's progress.

■ Remember the suggested duration for each Unit is a guide. It may well take longer. The important thing is that you are in control and will judge when it is time for the teaching and learning to move on.

Published by The Voices Foundation and Alfred Publishing Co
© The Voices Foundation 2014

Planning Template

THE VOICES FOUNDATION		FIRST STEPS: AGE 7-11
Year/Term:	Class:	Teacher:

Unit No/Focus:

Teaching Objectives:

Week One

Songs:

Listening/Video:

Teaching:

Week Two

Songs:

Listening/Video:

Teaching:

Week Three

Songs:

Listening/Video:

Teaching:

Week Four

Songs:

Listening/Video:

Teaching:

Assessment and Comments:

Published by The Voices Foundation and Alfred Publishing Co

Here is a completed plan for Unit 1

THE VOICES FOUNDATION		FIRST STEPS: AGE 7-11
Year/Term: 2014 Autumn	Class: Hawks	Teacher: Ms Raven

Unit No/Focus: 1

Singing Development

Teaching Objectives:

- To ensure each person 'finds' his/her Singing Voice
- To listen and to imitate song phrases
- To pitch-match the teacher, with others and another individual
- To sing as a class, group and as individuals

Week One

Songs: - Ev'ryone, good morning [Songs, 119] - Che che kule [Songs, 114] - Down by the ocean [Songs, 118] - Here I come [Songs, 124]

Listening/Video:

Teaching: - Teach Songs as per Set One and Set Two

Week Two

Songs: Songs from Week 1 PLUS - Say, boom, chicka boom [Songs, 147]

Listening/Video:

Teaching: - Revise Songs from Week 1 - Add new songs - Set One and Two - Set Three: pitch-matching

Week Three

Songs: - Previous songs PLUS - Oliver Twist [Songs, 138]

Listening/Video: - Badinerie

Teaching: - Add new songs - Set Three - Set Four - Set Five
- Assess understanding

Week Four

Songs:

Listening/Video:

Teaching:

Assessment and Comments:

- Songs seemed to be straightforward and learned well.
- Still some work needed to get all children to pitch-match.

Published by The Voices Foundation and Alfred Publishing Co

Here is a completed plan for Unit 12

THE VOICES FOUNDATION		FIRST STEPS: AGE 7-11
Year/Term: 2015 Summer	Class: Hawks	Teacher: Ms Raven

Unit No/Focus: 12

Performing: playing pitch [tuned] percussion

Teaching Objectives:
- To acquire basic co-ordination and playing skills on pitch percussion, eg xylophone, glockenspiel, chime bars
- To play several known song phrases
- To improvise melodic phrases on pitch percussion

Week One

Songs: – Ev'ryone, good morning [Songs, 119] – Fire! Fire! [Songs, 120] – Doggie, doggie [Songs, 116] – Here I come [Songs, 124]

Listening/Video: – YouTube 'How to play xylophone for beginners'

Teaching: – Need pitch percussion from store with pairs of beaters – Revise known songs – Teach new song – Set One

Week Two

Songs: – Fire! Fire! – Rain, rain, go away [Songs, 144] – Ev'ryone, good morning

Listening/Video: – YouTube 'How to play xylophone for beginners'

Teaching: – Need pitch percussion from store with pairs of beaters – Revise songs – Set Two – Set Three

Week Three

Songs: – All songs on the SONGS list

Listening/Video: – Toccata [track 87]

Teaching: – Need pitch percussion from store with pairs of beaters – Set Three – Set Four – Assess playing skills

Week Four Might need this week to ensure all have had enough opportunity to play

Songs:

Listening/Video:

Teaching:

Assessment and Comments:
- All children show ability to play one or more song phrases using two beaters with some alternating.
- Need another xylophone; some beaters are in poor condition.
- Class enjoyed the improvising.

Published by The Voices Foundation and Alfred Publishing Co
© The Voices Foundation 2014

The Stepping Stones

22 progressive steps of skills and concepts

Units 1–12 and Revision Unit A [1st year]

Let's start

Unit 1
Singing new songs
Pitch-matching

Unit 2
More songs
Listening and thinking
Pitch awareness

Unit 8
Pitch, dynamics, tempo
Thinking Voice

Unit 9
Untuned percussion
Spoken rhythm names

Unit 10
Singing tone-colour
Singing pitch names

Unit 11
Singing in tune
Listening and thinking
Rhythm and improvising

Published by The Voices Foundation and Alfred Publishing Co
© The Voices Foundation 2014

Singing Voice support
Pitch and dynamics

Thinking Voice
Vocal timbre

Untuned percussion skills
Instrumental timbre

Singing breath
Phrases

Song rhythms
Pulse
Metre

Onwards to
Year 2

Percussion playing skills
Playing known song phrases
Improvising

Revising Units 1 - 12
Assessing

Published by The Voices Foundation and Alfred Publishing Co
© The Voices Foundation 2014

Units 13-22 and Revision Unit B [2nd Year]

Year 2 starts here

Unit 13
- Comparing phrases
- Song tempo

Unit 18
- Singing tone-colour
- Stick notation

Unit 19
- Singing pitch names
- Time signatures and bar lines

Unit 20
- Rhythm: minim [half note]
- Singing pitch names
- Two-part singing [texture]

Unit 21
- Two-part music
- Tone-sets

Published by The Voices Foundation and Alfred Publishing Co
© The Voices Foundation 2014

Singing pitch names
Two-part singing [texture]

Pitch percussion
Rhythm notation

Legato singing
Phrase structure
Compose rhythm

Notation with noteheads
Rhythm sol-fa
Two-part singing [texture]

Finished!

Notation
New songs
Singing with expression

Revising Units 13 - 22

Published by The Voices Foundation and Alfred Publishing Co
© The Voices Foundation 2014

The National Curriculum [England]: Music programmes of study [2014]

First Steps: Age 7-11 supports the school in covering the requirements of the National Curriculum programmes of study.

Although *First Steps: Age 7-11* is for teachers and classes within KS2, it is a programme for newcomers to the education approach of *Inside Music*. It covers all the essentials of the KS1 requirements in order that the KS2 children can then move on with a secure foundation. The table illustrates how *First Steps* addresses the requirements of KS2 programmes of study, bearing in mind that it is intended as a two year course only, not four.

PROGRAMMES OF STUDY [SEPTEMBER 2014] KS1 * * See the introduction above	HOW *INSIDE MUSIC* SUPPORTS THE AIMS
Pupils should be taught to:	
use their voices expressively and creatively by singing songs and speaking chants and rhymes	The use of the voice is at the heart of *First Steps*. There are 69 songs and chants from which to choose. Most importantly, they help children in securing and understanding the Singing Voice and to grow confident in its use. In addition, the repertoire is used to develop an understanding of musical concepts, such as pulse, rhythm [NC: duration], pitch, dynamics and tempo, or as the National Curriculum describes them, the inter-related dimensions.
play tuned and untuned instruments musically	The playing of tuned [pitch] and untuned instruments is a continuous thread running throughout *First Steps*. The playing always arises out of a musical activity.
listen with concentration and understanding to a range of high-quality live and recorded music	A range of listening material is integrated seamlessly into *First Steps*. Careful use of questions helps to focus listening and develop appropriate musical understanding.
experiment with, create, select and combine sounds using the inter-related dimensions of music	Throughout *First Steps*, pupils are encouraged to work with the musical elements and use the terms of pulse, rhythm [duration], pitch, dynamics, timbre, phrase and tempo, once each is known and understood.

Published by The Voices Foundation and Alfred Publishing Co

PROGRAMMES OF STUDY [SEPTEMBER 2014] KS2 * * See the introduction above	HOW *INSIDE MUSIC* SUPPORTS THE AIMS
Pupils should be taught to sing and play musically with increasing confidence and control. They should develop an understanding of musical composition, organising and manipulating ideas within musical structures and reproducing sounds from aural memory.	
Pupils should be taught to:	
play and perform in solo and ensemble contexts, using their voices and playing musical instruments with increasing accuracy, control and expression	*First Steps* introduces pupils to singing skills: supportive posture, breath control, sound quality, singing in tune, legato singing, expressive considerations of song lyrics, appropriate tempo, dynamics and phrasing: Units 1, 2, 3, 4, 6, 10, 11, 13, 14, 17, 22 Opportunities for solo singing leadership are many and frequent. The pupils are introduced to two-part singing: Units 1, 2, 3, 4, 14, 15, 18, 20, 21 *First Steps* establishes the fundamentals of care, respect and techniques for playing untuned and tuned percussion. It provides opportunities for playing rhythm and melodic phrases, improvising and playing in two melodic parts: Units 5, 7, 9, 11, 12, 16, 17, 19, 20, 21
improvise and compose music for a range of purposes using the inter-related dimensions of music	*First Steps* sees improvising and composing as ways of using and reinforcing skills and knowledge and as a way for pupils to take ownership of their learning: Units 8, 11, 12, 13, 17, 19, 20
listen with attention to detail and recall sounds with increasing aural memory	*First Steps* gives importance to listening and thinking. For example: listening and imitating new song phrases; recalling known songs; activities that involve memory, recognition and identity of voice and instrument timbres; using the Thinking Voice in recall and creative activities. Units 1, 2, 4, 5, 7, 8, 11, 12, 13, 14, 17, 20, 22
use and understand staff and other musical notations	*First Steps* is a two-year programme introducing pupils to rhythm notation and rhythm sol-fa notation as precursors to learning about staff notation. Rhythm sol-fa is an ideal notation for singers to read and write. Units 14, 16, 17, 18, 19, 20, 22
appreciate and understand a wide range of high-quality live and recorded music drawn from different traditions and from great composers and musicians	*First Steps* includes 33 pieces of recorded music on CD-2 and various YouTube video suggestions. All the music is integral to the Teaching Objectives. There is music in the classical and jazz traditions and traditional music from Russia, Tibet and England. Among the great composers and musicians, there is Bach, Handel, Tchaikovsky, Britten, Lionel Hampton and Peter Donohoe. There is music for different styles of singing, music for solo instruments, small and large groups of players.
develop an understanding of the history of music	*First Steps* includes recorded examples of music from the 12th century and every century from the 16th through to the late 20th.

Published by The Voices Foundation and Alfred Publishing Co
© The Voices Foundation 2014

Published by The Voices Foundation and Alfred Publishing Co

The Teaching Programme

The Teaching Sequence

PAGE	UNIT	FOCUS	TEACHING OBJECTIVES
28	1	Singing Development	To ensure each person 'finds his/her Singing Voice'
			To listen to and imitate song phrases
			To pitch-match the teacher, another individual or the class
			To sing as a class, group and as individuals
31	2	Performing: singing Listening and thinking Concept: pitch	To add further songs and games
			To raise awareness of pitch
			To be able to identify known-song melody
			To listen to recorded music with purpose
32	3	Singing Development Concepts: pitch, dynamics	To develop aspects of singing posture
			To further an awareness of pitch change
			To raise an awareness of dynamics
36	4	Listening and thinking Concept: timbre	To establish the Thinking Voice
			To raise awareness of sound qualities [timbre] in the human voice
37	5	Performing: instruments Concept: timbre	To establish the fundamentals of care and technique when using untuned percussion
			To identify different instruments by sound quality only
41	6	Singing Development Concept: phrase	To recognise the start, duration and end of phrases
			To understand the singing breath
			To achieve singing with one breath per song phrase
43	7	Concepts: rhythm, pulse, metre	To perform the rhythms of individual song phrases
			To feel and mark the pulse as a consequence of rhythm
			To distinguish between rhythm and pulse
			To feel a repetitive cycle of four pulses in songs and recorded music: the metre of 4 beats
45	8	Listening and thinking Concepts: pitch, dynamics, tempo, phrase	To learn that:
			Pitch levels can be compared as being higher or lower
			Dynamic levels can be compared as being louder or quieter
			Tempos [speeds] can be compared as being faster or slower
			To develop the experience of using the Thinking Voice
48	9	Performing: playing Concept: rhythm [NC England: duration]	To learn to play song rhythms on untuned percussion
			To understand the basic principles of simple time rhythm
			To learn to use spoken rhythm names for simple time

Published by The Voices Foundation and Alfred Publishing Co
© The Voices Foundation 2014

PAGE	UNIT	FOCUS	TEACHING OBJECTIVES
51	10	Singing Development Concepts: pitch, timbre	To raise a general awareness of Singing Voice sound qualities To develop an understanding of and skills to influence the singing of vowels To listen to pitch changes in song phrases and to show the melodic line through hand movement To listen to a specific interval [pitch distance] between two levels of pitch in song melody To learn to recognise the interval with singing-names [solfa]: **soh** for the higher pitch, **me** for the lower pitch To learn to associate **soh** and **me** with their supporting handsigns
54	11	Singing Development Listening and thinking Concept: rhythm	To increase the accuracy and stability of pitch when singing: 'singing in tune' To listen to recorded pieces with purpose To identify a song from only its performed rhythm To develop early skills in improvising
57	12	Performing: playing pitch [tuned] percussion	To acquire basic co-ordination and playing skills on pitch percussion, eg xylophone, glockenspiel, chime bars To play several known song phrases To improvise melodic phrases on pitch percussion
60	REVISION UNIT A	Singing Development Performing: singing, playing instruments Concepts: pitch, rhythm, pulse, phrase, tempo, dynamics, timbre	To reinforce and assess skills, knowledge and understanding in the areas of singing development, performing, listening and concepts, acquired during the teaching of Units 1 - 12
64	13	Concepts: phrase, tempo	To compare the phrases of a known song as being the same or different To show that phrases in the same song can be of different lengths To show that tempo [speed] is important to the character of the song
67	14	Singing Development Concepts: pitch, rhythm	To further develop the sound quality of singing To be able to control the starting pitch of a song To be able to use 'stick notation' for **ta** [crotchet/ quarter note symbol] and **teh-teh** [two quaver/eighth notes symbol] To read and notate 'stick notation'

Published by The Voices Foundation and Alfred Publishing Co
© The Voices Foundation 2014

PAGE	UNIT	FOCUS	TEACHING OBJECTIVES
70	15	Performing: two-part singing Concept: pitch	To add a third singing name, **lah**, to **soh** and **me** To work aurally with **lah soh me** [l-s-m] with supporting handsigns To improvise pitch using **lah soh me** To introduce the early stages leading to two-part singing
74	16	Performing: pitch [tuned] percussion Concepts: pitch, rhythm	To play on pitch percussion phrases from known songs To introduce the **ta rest** [crotchet/quarter note rest] To read and notate rhythm phrases that include the **rest** symbol, **Z**
77	17	Singing Development Concept: phrase structure	To sing with sustained sounds that connect smoothly and easily To identify, count and label phrases in songs [structure] To compose rhythm pieces
80	18	Performing: two-part music Notation	To read and perform rhythm notation using noteheads To sing music with two parts [texture] To combine rhythm and pitch symbols to produce melodic notation known as rhythm sol-fa
83	19	Notation Concept: pitch	To introduce **doh** and to work aurally with **s-m-d** To use the tone-set **s-m-d** when improvising, memorising and reading [rhythm sol-fa] To understand bar lines and time signatures
88	20	Performing: two-part singing Concepts: pitch, rhythm	To introduce the minim [half note] rhythm value To perform two-part music: song melody with melodic *ostinato* To introduce and use the note **ray** To use the tone-set **m-r-d**, to sing song phrases, read rhythm sol-fa, to use memory and recall and to improvise
92	21	Performing: two-part singing, two-part pitch percussion playing Concept: pitch	To sing music with two voice parts To work vocally and with pitch instruments on tone-sets formed from l-s-m-r-d To play song phrases on pitch percussion To play music with two instrumental parts [texture] To be able to perform, listen out for and understand the music device known as *drone*

Published by The Voices Foundation and Alfred Publishing Co
© The Voices Foundation 2014

PAGE	UNIT	FOCUS	TEACHING OBJECTIVES
96	22	Performing: singing Notation	To read, sing and learn a new song using notation To learn and perform new songs To sing songs with attention to technique and expression
99	REVISION UNIT B	Singing Development Performing: singing and playing Concepts: pitch, dynamics, tempo, phrase, rhythm, pulse Notation	To reinforce and assess the skills, knowledge and understanding in the areas of singing development, performing, listening, notation and concepts, acquired during the teaching of Units 13 - 22

Published by The Voices Foundation and Alfred Publishing Co
© The Voices Foundation 2014

FOCUS

- Singing Development

TEACHING OBJECTIVES

- To ensure each person 'finds' his/her Singing Voice
- To listen to and imitate song phrases
- To pitch-match the teacher, another individual or the class
- To sing as a class, group and as individuals

WHAT IS GOING TO HAPPEN?

- Establishing a routine for teaching songs
- Establishing a routine for a secure collective start to singing
- Singing as an individual within a group activity

SONGS

Call-and-response song:

Ev'ryone, good morning [page 119]

Echo chant/song:

Che che kule [page 114]

Say, boom, chicka boom [page 147]

Songs for individual activity:

Down by the ocean [page 118]

Here I come [page 124]

Lots of rosy apples [page 134] *

Singing game:

Oliver Twist [page 138]

HOT SONG

LISTENING

Badinerie - Bach [track 70]

GENERAL GUIDANCE

Focus on lots of singing and musical activity.

Work to establish and develop confidence, collective and individual.

Establish clear routines for teaching new songs [indicated by the *italics*]

Establish a clear routine for starting known songs

Teach 'little-and-often'; think quality; enjoy!

It is possible that not all children have found their Singing Voice and are using their speaking voice. A 'wrong habit' can be a problem to sort out, but with these cases a threefold strategy is recommended:

1. Thinking higher: singing out of the top of the head!

2. Opportunities to sing without others

3. Listening to and imitating another child

If there is a game or actions to a song, it will be described on the song page; it is advised that children have opportunities to play the game or incorporate any actions: it will give enjoyment and context for the music and help to secure it in the memory.

Published by The Voices Foundation and Alfred Publishing Co
© The Voices Foundation 2014

SET ONE Teaching a new song routine

The teacher first learns the song to be taught, perhaps with the help of the recording on CD-1

Teaching 'Ev'ryone, good morning'

- You sing phrase 1 as class listens; class imitates as you listen; repeat the process

- You sing phrase 2 as class listens; class imitates as you listen; repeat the process

- You sing phrase 1 and class responds with phrase 2; repeat the process

It can be helpful to show with one hand who is meant to be singing

This greeting could be used as a regular welcome in class

SET TWO Echo the leader

In an echo song or chant, the leader performs a musical phrase that is then echoed by others

Teaching 'Say, boom, chicka boom'

- Speak each phrase rhythmically; class echoes

- Whisper each phrase rhythmically; class echoes

- Speak with a quiet volume; class echoes

- Speak with a louder volume for phrase 1, then less loud for each succeeding phrase; class mirrors each volume

- Speak with a higher pitched voice; then a lower pitched voice

- Using the Singing Voice, spontaneously make-up singing sounds for each phrase; the melody can vary from phrase to phrase

Later, there could well be individuals who would wish to lead the class with this activity

Teaching 'Che che kule'

- You sing phrase 1 as class listens; class imitates as you listen; repeat the process

- Teach the other phrases in the same way

- You sing all five phrases separately with each immediately followed by a class echo; repeat the process

- This is also an action song: see the Song page

SET THREE Pitch-matching the leader

Tell the children that the game is 'finding' the leader's Singing Voice up in the 'pitch tree'- a game of singing tag!

Any singable starting pitch is acceptable, but do encourage yourself and the children-leaders towards higher pitch and away from the pitch of the speaking voice

Teach the song: 'Lots of rosy apples' or 'Here I come' or 'Down by the ocean'

- Ideally sing the complete song to the class, then use the **SET ONE** routine

- When the song melody and words are secure, use the following routine to ensure a collective start to a selected pitch and speed:

  - The first time a song is revisited in the lesson, you sing the song to remind the children; they listen

  - You then sing on the starting pitch to a firm rhythm and tempo [speed]: *"Off you go"*; the class sings the song; you listen

- 'Lots of rosy apples': the individual sets the pitch and tempo in singing phrases 1 and 2; the class should match the leader in phrases 3 and 4

- 'Here I come': the leader sets the pitch and tempo and the class or another individual or group should match

- 'Down by the ocean': here the individuals must match the pitch used in the song so far

SET FOUR Singing game

A Singing Game is traditionally a street or playground game between several children in which a made-up song is part of the process

With some action games, it is helpful and motivating for the class if the complete song and its actions are first demonstrated

Teach 'Oliver Twist'

- Ask the class to imagine they each have a 'shadow partner' facing them

- You sing phrase 1 and include the actions outlined in the Song page; class imitates; repeat as necessary to secure

- Teach phrase 2 and include actions; repeat as necessary to secure

- Sing the song with 'shadow' partners with enough repetition to gain familiarity

- Play the game as outlined on the Song page

SET FIVE Listening to Badinerie

Read the background notes for this piece in the Listening Material pages

Listen to 'Badinerie'

- The class listens with no introduction to the piece

- Before a repeat hearing, ask the children to find something that they can tell you afterwards about 'Badinerie'

- Then ask them to listen out for a specific feature, perhaps named by a child eg the solo instrument, the speed, the volume, the repeating structure - and replay

LEARNING OUTCOMES

- Children will have learned a number of new songs

- Children will have an understood routine for learning a new song

- They will have an understood way for starting a known song

- They are pitch-matching the leader and the established pitch

- Confidence is being established for individual singing

- Children can listen with purpose to recorded music

Published by The Voices Foundation and Alfred Publishing Co
© The Voices Foundation 2014

Three weeks

FOCUS

- Performing: singing
- Listening and thinking
- Concept: pitch

TEACHING OBJECTIVES

- To add further songs and games
- To raise awareness of pitch
- To be able to identify known-song melody
- To listen to recorded music with purpose

WHAT IS GOING TO HAPPEN?

- Singing songs requiring a leader
- Repeating a song to a new pitch level [higher / lower]
- Identifying a known song from its hummed melody
- Listening to recorded music with a defined activity

SONGS

For pitch awareness:

Chest, chest, knee, toe [page 114]

High, low, chickalow [page 126]

We can sing high [page 153]

Songs requiring a leader:

Brown bread and butter O [page 110]

Salut! Ça va? [page 147]

HOT SONG

Oo-a-lay-lay [page 139]

LISTENING

Le Coucou - Daquin [track 71]

GENERAL GUIDANCE

Learning new songs develops the children's listening, concentration and memory and also provides them with essential experiences which the teaching can draw upon in order to develop their musicianship.

Pitch is that unseen element of music that when we are singing, we can only sense. The brain has to work on that sense impression in order to rationalise what is happening. Drawing children's attention to the variability of pitch is the first stage in understanding and defining pitch.

A melody is largely defined by the organisation of its pitch and rhythm elements: hence we recognise a tune by its distinctive pitch and rhythm patterns.

When playing recorded music, it is helpful for the children to be given a listening focus. This is usually suggested in the Teaching Ideas.

Published by The Voices Foundation and Alfred Publishing Co
© The Voices Foundation 2014

SET ONE Songs to boost individual performing experience

With all new songs, use the established routines and take time to establish familiarity

Teach 'Salut! Ça va?' and 'Brown bread and butter O'

'Salut! Ça va?' is a simple greeting with response in French

- For the question and answer phrases, there are a number of performing combinations:

  - you + class

  - you + child

  - child + you

  - child + child

  - child + class

  Each of these will demand pitch-matching from the 'answer'and gives lots of opportunities to develop individual singing confidence

In 'Brown bread and butter O', the challenge is for the selected child to mentally choose the new name before singing phrase 4

SET TWO Songs to help raise awareness of pitch

Teach the songs: 'Chest, chest, knee, toe' 'High, low, chickalow' 'We can sing high'

It is suggested that the songs are taught on separate occasions

The pitch movement of 'Chest, chest, knee, toe' is helped by the actions to be found on the Song page

'High, low, chickalow': again the suggested actions between pairs give a strong clue to the movement up and down of the singing pitch

In 'We can sing high', the words 'high' and 'low' are descriptive of the singing pitch at those points in the melody

SET THREE Listening out for the two-note cuckoo song

Each of the listening items in this programme is given a background in the Listening Material pages; this can be useful for you and the children to know

It could be helpful to check that the class is aware of the cuckoo and its song

'Le coucou'

The cuckoo is busy flying and calling from all over the wood. Can the children count how many times they hear the cuckoo's call? What else did they discover?

SET FOUR A Hot Song

Teach 'Oo-a-lay-lay'

This echo song could be performed using the ideas suggested for 'Say, boom, chicka boom', Unit 1, SET TWO

It is an action song - see the Song page

- Individual children show greater willingness to be leaders in the singing

- Children understand that pitch is associated with the 'highness' and 'lowness' of the Singing Voice

- Given something specific to focus on, children listen with concentration to recorded music

Published by The Voices Foundation and Alfred Publishing Co
© The Voices Foundation 2014

FOCUS

- Singing Development
- Concepts: pitch, dynamics

TEACHING OBJECTIVES

- To develop aspects of singing posture
- To further an awareness of pitch change
- To raise an awareness of dynamics

WHAT IS GOING TO HAPPEN?

- Using postures, standing and sitting, that support the singing voice
- Responding to pitch change in known songs
- Controlling the volume [the dynamic] of the Singing Voice
- Listening to recorded music that features changes in the dynamics

SONGS

Songs for demonstrating starting pitch changes:

Ev'ryone, good morning [page 119]

Lots of rosy apples [page 134] *

Oo-a-lay-lay [page 139]

Salut! Ça va? [page 147]

Songs to demonstrate pitch change within the melody:

Bow wow wow [page 110]

Goblins are around tonight [page 121]

High, low, chickalow [page 126]

Rain on the green grass [page 143] *

Songs to show control of dynamics

Engine, engine [page 118]

Goblins are around tonight [page 121]

Oo-a-lay-lay [page 139]

HOT SONG

Tony Chestnut [page 152]

LISTENING

Parade - Ibert [track 72]

GENERAL GUIDANCE

Singing stems from the exhalation of air in the lungs. Posture that assists the breath control and supports the Singing Voice is of considerable importance. The muscles around the diaphragm need to have maximum freedom. A balanced standing or sitting position will aid this, whereas sitting cross-legged on the floor will impede the diaphragm.

Song melody can be sung at more than one pitch level. In successive performances of a song, the starting pitch can be adjusted higher or lower.

Each successive note in a melody will either be a repeat pitch or go to a higher or lower pitch. When the latter takes place the pitch difference can vary, perhaps a small difference, perhaps large. The pitch distance between two consecutive notes is called an interval.

Children will have a clear understanding of the concept of loud and quiet. Volume, or to use the music term, dynamic[s], is largely used as an expressive element in music and causes an emotional response in the listener. Being able to control dynamics in singing will aid the impact of performance. Dynamics depend on unrestricted diaphragm muscles and airflow. So once again supportive posture is essential.

SET ONE Singing Development: supportive posture

It is usually advisable to plan Singing Development activities for the start of a music lesson

Singing is about the mind and the whole body

Standing posture

- With balanced body, fully raise the arms above the head, pause, then let the muscles become slack and the body hang loose like a string puppet or rag-doll

- Imagine the slack strings are gradually made taut and the body becomes upright once more; arms are loose at the side, shoulders relaxed; the legs and knees are 'soft', not tensed; the head is level and the eyes are alert

- Sing a known song, such as 'High, low, chickalow'

Sitting posture

- Sitting forward on the front half of the chair, feet flat on the ground, hands on legs

- An alert body is allowed to collapse at the waist [slouch]; each child takes one hand behind their back just above the waist and presses the spine inwards [the re-set button]; hand comes back to the front; shoulders relaxed; the head is level and the eyes are alert

- Sing a known song such as 'Ev'ryone, good morning [afternoon]'

SET TWO Using actions to show pitch change in melody

Teach / revise the songs 'Rain on the green grass', 'Bow wow wow', 'Goblins are around tonight', 'High, low, chickalow'

The following are ideas that can be used with any of the songs

Accuracy of the actions is sought, but the mental process is just as important

The better known the song, the better the responses will be

- All the children sing the song and:

  - move their arms according to the rising and falling pattern of the pitch

  - with a finger trace in the air from left to right the contour of the melody

  - one child traces with a marker on a board the contour of the song; retaining this, the song is sung again and second person traces; the two are compared

Published by The Voices Foundation and Alfred Publishing Co
© The Voices Foundation 2014

SET THREE Demonstrating dynamics when singing

Supportive standing posture will enable the singers to control the dynamics more easily: see **SET ONE**

Teach / revise 'Engine, engine' 'Goblins are around tonight'

These Teaching Ideas can be used with either song

Be aware that loud singing and quiet singing should always retain a singing tone. A shouting tone and a whispering tone are very different to singing

- Sing the song quietly

- Sing the song more loudly

- Sing phrases alternately quieter and louder

- Start the song very quietly and very gradually increase the volume until the last few notes are being sung more loudly

- The above idea but with reverse dynamics

- The class sings a song at "Level 1" - very quietly; then "Level 4" - loudly; the class is then divided into two equal groupings; group A is secretly shown a card with a number - 1, 2, 3 or 4. They sing the song at the dynamic that they collectively believe to be representative of that number; after, group B attempts to identify the number; the answer is then revealed

Teach / revise and sing 'Oo-a-lay-lay'

This is an echo song in which each phrase sung by the leader is imitated by the rest

- The class must identify the dynamic used by the leader and use it in their echo; the leader may change the dynamic from phrase to phrase; the leader may comment on whether the class responded accurately to his/her intentions; the class should be made aware that the volume range for one singer is not as great as that for a large group

SET FOUR Recorded music with changing dynamics

Without telling the class the intentions of the composer, Jacques Ibert, when composing 'Parade', ask them to listen to the track and after to comment on the dynamics. What does the music suggest is happening?

LEARNING OUTCOMES

- Children show that posture is important to the act of singing and breath control

- Children are increasingly aware of the rise and fall of pitch that takes place in a melody

- Children are aware that the dynamics of musical sound varies and can be controlled when singing

Published by The Voices Foundation and Alfred Publishing Co
© The Voices Foundation 2014

Two weeks

FOCUS

- Listening and thinking
- Concept: timbre

TEACHING OBJECTIVES

- To establish the Thinking Voice
- To raise awareness of sound qualities [timbre] in the human voice

WHAT IS GOING TO HAPPEN?

- Learning how to use the memory and thinking to 'hear' the inner Singing Voice, the Thinking Voice
- Learning through songs to recognise and identify differences in the sound qualities of voices

SONGS

For establishing the Thinking Voice:

Chest, chest, knee, toe [page 114]

Engine, engine [page 118]

Hill an' gully ride-a [page 127]

I heard, I heard the old man say [page 130]

For considering vocal timbre:

Doggie, doggie [page 116] *

Down by the ocean [page 118]

HOT CHANT

Double, double [page 117]

LISTENING

YouTube: 'Swing low, sweet chariot' – compare Paul Robeson, Johnny Cash, The King's Singers, Eric Clapton, Kathleen Battle with Harlem Boys Choir

GENERAL GUIDANCE

The Thinking Voice enables us to record, recall, create and, above all, be musicians.

Just as we can recall a familiar voice or song or recall the memory of what has been said in our heads, so the musical memory works in a similar way. The Thinking Voice enables us to internalise a new song and, for example, recall how the rhythm of a melody goes. If we have the skills and knowledge to read and write down musical notation, then the Thinking Voice enables us to notate what we can recall or what we hear in our aural-mind, ie compose.

Singing is at the heart of learning, for it is the Thinking Voice 'live'.

Timbre [pronounce: *tam*-bre] is a word used in music to talk about the tone or sound quality of a voice or instrument. The components of a sound are several eg materials, how the sound is created and the sound's overtone content. The differences enable us to define the sound with such words as dark, bright, harsh, warm. Without seeing the source of the sound, it is possible to identify even small differences in sound quality. Where the sound has been heard before and given a name, then the memory may trigger its identity.

Hot Tip 1 New songs: continue to use the teaching routine given in Unit 1.

Hot Tip 2 Known songs: continue to give a firm and rhythmic *"Off you go!"* on the starting pitch.

Hot Tip 3 Consider:

- encouraging individual children to take on the role of 'Starter'
- changing the starting pitch and tempo [speed] for repeats of a song, it refreshes the song and the singers

Published by The Voices Foundation and Alfred Publishing Co
© The Voices Foundation 2014

SET ONE Hearing sounds in our head: the Thinking Voice

Associated activities learned with a song will trigger the aural memory even when no sound is made

Teach / revise 'Chest, Chest, knee, toe' or 'I heard, I heard the old man say'

- The song is sung several times with its associated actions - see the relevant Song page

- The song is 'sung' with the help of the memory <u>inside the head</u> only as the actions are performed, ie silent singing

Teach 'Hill an' gully ride-a'

- Each child sings with a regular tap using the right hand on the left side of the chest to mark the pulse, the 'heartbeat' of the song

- As above, but the children 'silent sing', using the Thinking Voice for each 'Hill an' gully' response-refrain

Teach / revise 'Engine, engine'

- 'Engine, engine' is sung to a steady tapped pulse to mark the heartbeat of the song and immediately repeated [twice through]

- As above, but this time you suggest that the engine will pass through several tunnels during which the singing will not be heard, but continues with the Thinking Voice and a quiet tapped 'heartbeat' pulse; the tunnels are indicated by placing a hand on your head for the duration of each phrase you choose to be a 'tunnel'; the phrases are indicated on the relevant Song page by a phrase mark:

TIP! The 'on and off' of the hand signal needs to take place a moment before the beginning or end of the phrase

SET TWO Vocal timbre [pronounce: *tam-bre*]

Teach / revise 'Doggie, doggie' or 'Down by the ocean'

The games for these songs are given on the relevant Song pages; they give the children focused listening on the finer sound qualities of familiar voices

YouTube singing of 'Swing low, sweet chariot'

Go to YouTube search and type in 'Swing low, sweet chariot' and hopefully, videos/recordings of the singers listed under Listening will be available.

- Let the class hear each to compare the sound qualities of contrasting voices singing the same song; ask them to comment and compare the qualities of vocal sound - the timbre

- Children are aware of their inner-singing voice - the Thinking Voice - when recalling familiar melodic phrases

- Children can switch backwards and forwards from the Singing Voice and the Thinking Voice

- Just using sound information only, children can aurally detect large and small differences of timbre between singers

Two weeks

FOCUS

- Performing: instruments
- Concept: timbre

TEACHING OBJECTIVES

- To establish the fundamentals of care and technique when using untuned percussion
- To identify different instruments by sound quality [timbre] only

WHAT IS GOING TO HAPPEN?

- Teaching care and respect for instruments
- Using correct terminology for instruments
- Developing holding requirements and playing techniques
- Memorising the sound qualities of several instruments

SONGS

Double, double [page 117]

Engine, engine [page 118]

Down by the ocean [page 118]

Hill an' gully ride-a [page 127]

Che che kule [page 114]

HOT SONG

Peel Bananas [page 141]

LISTENING

The Clog Dance - Hertel/Lanchbery [track 73]

YouTube: The Clog Dance - Royal Ballet video

The Bird, Duck and Cat from 'Peter and the Wolf' - Prokofiev [tracks 74, 75, 76]

GENERAL GUIDANCE

A music-teaching programme will have a purposeful role for instruments. Playing skills should be acknowledged and imparted to pupils. Respect and care of instruments will ensure their long life [see SET ONE].

Each instrument has its own identifiable sound quality and its own name.

As a result of materials and construction, instruments of the same name can vary enormously. Generally speaking poor quality materials and construction result in poor sound and shorter life. Children deserve the best tone quality if they are to take an interest in using instruments.

Percussion is just one family of instruments, those that are struck or shaken to make a sound. They are sub-divided into unturned percussion, those that do not play melody, and tuned [or pitch] percussion that can.

Instruments can strike terror into the heart of the bravest of teachers because they are associated with uncontrollable noise. If a certain strategy is adopted and some basic ground rules are adopted, then this fear need not materialise.

For illustrations of instruments, the Google search engine is a tremendous asset. Equally YouTube videos are a rich source for showing instruments that are relevant to this programme being played.

There may be pupils, colleagues and members of the community who are willing to bring examples of instruments featured in this programme to show and possibly illustrate their sound to your class.

Published by The Voices Foundation and Alfred Publishing Co
© The Voices Foundation 2014

SET ONE Introduce the untuned percussion instruments

When using untuned percussion, think: fewer instruments; shorter time; frequent use; use proper names; quieter playing!

Have single examples of several different instruments in good condition

For hand-held instruments that are struck, the preferred hand does the striking

For larger and heavier hand-held instruments that are struck, it might be appropriate for the weight to be supported by the knee or floor

Maracas should be used in pairs, one to each hand

When using a beater or stick to strike the instrument remember that the resulting sound quality will reflect the type of hardness of the beater or stick head, so have a small variety available

Instruments deserve careful storage; avoid placing in direct sunlight or near heaters

- Introduce each instrument in turn with its proper name and demonstrate how to hold and strike

- Tell the class about care and storage of instruments

SET TWO Warm-up to playing untuned percussion

Class should sit with an upright posture on chairs with both feet comfortably placed on the floor

- Class shake wrists gently above the upper legs

- Using the same loose wrists, class tap their upper legs with open palms

- To a steady count of 1 2 3 4 from you, the children:

  - tap both hands on upper legs simultaneously

  - tap alternately left - right upper legs

  - right hand only taps 4 times, left hand taps left leg 4 times - repeat several times to establish the pattern

  - alternate right hand x 2, left hand x 2 pattern

  - alternate right hand x 2, left hand x 4 pattern

  - tap with alternate hands on left upper leg x 4, right upper leg x 4 pattern

- Build a sequence of changing patterns from the above

- Let pairs of children devise their own sequence and perform to the class

SET THREE Using untuned percussion in music-making

Sing 'Engine, engine'; chant 'Double, double'

- Select an instrument to play steady pulse to the singing / chanting

- Select four instruments; assign one instrument to each phrase to play a steady pulse to the singing / chanting

- As above, but the instruments play the rhythm [following the pattern of the words]

Sing 'Hill an' gully ride-a' 'Down by the ocean'

- Select an instrument to play the rhythm of each response phrase, 'Hill an' gully', as the song is sung

- For each of the response phrases, 'Hill an' gully', assign a different instrument to play the rhythm as the song is sung

- Select two different instruments and assign one each to play the solo phrases, 'I told Ma' and 'I told Pa' in 'Down by the ocean'; at these points the 'singing' is done by Thinking Voice [silent singing]

Sing 'Che, che, kule'

- With two singing groups, A performs the 'lead' phrases and B the echoes; as each group sings, it marks the pulse, group A tapping the upper legs, group B tapping the palm of the hands

- As above, but with two individuals singing and playing with two different instruments

SET FOUR Instrumental timbre [playing]

Each instrument has its own proper name and distinctive timbre

- Three instruments are selected and placed out of sight; a child is asked to select one and briefly play it: *"What is the name of the instrument?"*

- Four instruments are selected and placed out of sight; a child plays two consecutively or simultaneously: *"What are the names of the instruments?"*

Published by The Voices Foundation and Alfred Publishing Co
© The Voices Foundation 2014

SET FIVE Instrumental timbre [recorded sound]

Recorded Listening: 'Clog Dance' 'The Bird, Duck and Cat'

'Clog Dance': In this scene from a ballet story, the Widow Simone attempts to dance in a pair of wooden clogs; there is a YouTube video of the Royal Ballet performing this - great fun to watch!

☐ Play this excerpt asking the class to identify the sound of the wooden clogs and counting how many attempts the Widow Simone makes to dance in them

'Peter and the Wolf' excerpts: the Bird is represented by the flute; the Duck by the oboe; the Cat by the clarinet; these are wind instruments ie each is blown to produce sound

☐ First excerpt: the bird is heard

☐ Second excerpt: both the duck and the bird are heard; when?

☐ Third excerpt: the cat is about, but so are the duck and bird; what is happening?

☐ For the third excerpt have three groups, one for each of the three instruments; the group raise their hands on hearing their instrument and lower when it can no longer be heard. Listen again, but each group is on the 'look out' for a different instrument

LEARNING OUTCOMES

☐ Children accept responsibility for the care of school instruments

☐ Children can identify the timbre of some untuned percussion instruments and use proper names

☐ Children show supportive posture and handling skills when using untuned percussion instruments

☐ When performing on untuned percussion, children are able to show skill and accuracy

☐ When listening to recorded music, children can identify individual sounds and instruments

Published by The Voices Foundation and Alfred Publishing Co
© The Voices Foundation 2014

FOCUS

- Singing Development
- Concept: phrase

TEACHING OBJECTIVES

- To recognise the start, duration and end of phrases
- To understand the singing-breath
- To achieve singing with one breath per song phrase

WHAT IS GOING TO HAPPEN?

- Two groups alternately singing the phrases of a song
- Using actions to identify the duration of phrases in songs
- Learning how to be aware of the singing-breath
- Learning when to breathe in songs
- Identifying the duration of phrases in recorded instrumental music

SONGS

Brown bread and butter O [page 110]

Button you must wander [page 112]

Goblins are around tonight [page 121]

Lots of rosy apples [page 134] *

Summer goodbye [page 151]

Suo gân [page 152]

We can sing high [page 153]

HOT SONG

LISTENING

The Swan - Saint-Saëns [track 77]

GENERAL GUIDANCE

A phrase is a stage on a melodic or rhythmic journey: a phrase sets out, travels and arrives. Usually a melody or rhythm piece is a series of phrases, the last one giving a sense of finality.

The duration or length of a phrase can vary from melody to melody and sometimes within a melody.

Singing Development: essentially the Singing Voice is a wind instrument; the source of singing sound is air exhaled. Inhaling and exhaling is natural to us. In singing we need to manage the air exhaled across the membranes of the vocal cords in the larynx to make sound.

In singing we manage the breathing process with the phrases of the melody. Singers breathe before and after each phrase in a song, although breathing after every other phrase may be better if the phrases are short.

Notated songs will often show the phrase length with a phrase mark:

Hot Tip 1: when the class is using actions as part of their singing, the teacher is best able to assess and see where help is needed when standing outside the area of action.

Hot Tip 2: when the class performs, the teacher listens and vice-versa.

SET ONE Identifying the start, duration and end of song phrases

Sing 'Lots of rosy apples' or 'We can sing high'

The relevant Song pages will show the start, duration and end of phrases in these songs with phrase marks:

- Class sings and identifies the phrases by using one 'rainbow' arm arcing across the front of the body per phrase; see the Song pages; 'Lots of rosy apples' has four equal length phrases; 'We can sing high' has two equal length phrases

- Two groups alternately sing the song phrases

SET TWO Singing Development: breath control

With fingertips of one hand sitting on the tummy and the other hand flat on the spine at the same level, the class blows away any air they have and experiences muscles contracting like a belt tightening; ask them to hold very briefly the 'nil-breath', before 'releasing the belt' and experiencing the new intake of air into the lungs

'Breathing with the phrase' is a useful guide to intake and length of exhalation; where necessary, phrase marks are shown in the written notation; see the relevant Song pages

Sing 'Lots of rosy apples' or 'Goblins are about tonight'

- Class identifies the phrases by using one 'rainbow' arm movement across the front of the body per phrase; see the Song pages; each song has four phrases

- An easy intake of breath is made before each new phrase; there is no need to fill the lungs

Singers should not breathe during the phrase and the longer sounding notes should be sustained

Class identifies the phrases by using one 'rainbow' arm arcing across the front of the body per phrase; see the Song pages; 'Suo gân' has four equal length phrases; 'Summer goodbye' has six equal length phrases

Work as before

SET THREE Phrase in recorded listening

'The Swan' written by Camille Saint-Saëns as part of his 'Carnival of the Animals', represents the grace of the swan with an equally graceful melody played by a cello and accompanied by a piano

- As the piece is played the children identify the start, duration and end of each phrase using 'rainbow' arc movements or through other actions of the arms or body

- Small groupings or pairs or individuals devise an expressive dance that illustrates the length [duration] of some or all of the phrases

- Children are aware that melody is structured as several individual phrases

- Children can identify and demonstrate the start, duration and finish of a song phrase through movement

- Children are aware of the phrase mark

- Children understand that in their singing they use one sustained breath per melodic phrase

Published by The Voices Foundation and Alfred Publishing Co

Three weeks

FOCUS

Concepts: rhythm, pulse, metre

TEACHING OBJECTIVES

To perform the rhythms of individual song phrases

To feel and mark the pulse as a consequence of rhythm

To distinguish between rhythm and pulse

To feel a repetitive cycle of four pulses in songs and recorded music: the metre of 4 beats

WHAT IS GOING TO HAPPEN?

As separate activities, song rhythms are tapped and the resulting pulse is marked

Rhythm and pulse are simultaneously tapped and marked

Children perform songs and actions with a 4-beat repetitive sequence

Songs are performed with visual and instrumental support

Recorded music with a 4-beat metre is heard

SONGS

Goblins are around tonight [page 121]

I like coffee, I like tea [page 131]

Obwisana [page 136]

Plainie clappie [page 142]

Spinning top [page 149]

HOT SONG

How many miles to Babylon? [page 128]

LISTENING

Viennese Musical Clock - Kodály [track 78]

March - Tchaikovsky [track 79]

'Where are you?' – Traditional Russian [track 80]

GENERAL GUIDANCE

The word *rhythm* is ultimately derived from the ancient Greek *rhuthmos* - flow. Music is organised to flow as a series of sounds. The sounds usually have a pattern to them that sets up a 'time-motion', sensed by our minds and bodies as a regular pulsation. The rhythmic patterns and pulsation together can bring about another pattern, a pattern of stronger and weaker pulses, known as metre. So, pulsation that is felt as a repetitive pattern of **strong** - *weak* - *weak* - *weak* is said to have a metre of four *beats*.

In this programme all new concept learning stems from the children's experiences of making music, largely singing songs and choral music. The teaching uses these songs and experiences to lead the children towards new skills, understanding and knowledge. This in turn will enable children to access music reading and writing.

Hot Tip: Children usually understand better when they are actively 'doing' the music, and not talking about it.

Published by The Voices Foundation and Alfred Publishing Co
© The Voices Foundation 2014

SET ONE Securing the songs

Teach the listed songs and play any associated games [see Song pages] ensuring that the class is very familiar and comfortable with them.

Teach with the 'good practice' routine advocated in Unit 1

SET TWO Rhythm

Class sings one of the songs from this list:

- Goblins are around tonight
- *I like coffee, I like tea*
- *Plainie clappie*
- *Spinning top*

It is suggested that for rhythmic accuracy and reasonable volume each child taps with two fingers of the preferred hand on the other, stationary palm

To support their efforts, you play an untuned percussion instrument eg claves

- Class sings the words of phrase 1, simultaneously tapping the word pattern
- Speak phrase 1, simultaneously tapping the word pattern
- Using just the Thinking Voice for phrase 1, class taps the word pattern
- Several children or an individual tap the phrase on untuned percussion as the rest listen
- Select other phrases from these songs and follow the same teaching routine

SET THREE Pulse

Class sings one of the songs from this list:

- Goblins are around tonight
- *I like coffee, I like tea*
- *Plainie clappie*
- *Spinning top*
- Using the *"Off you go!"* routine, the class sings the song, quietly marking the regular pulsation felt from the singing [the 'heartbeat']; you play an untuned instrument, eg a tambour, in time with the pulse

It is possible that some children will tap the rhythm of the song and not mark the pulse; if this happens, it is suggested that just before the song is sung you speak at regular and steady tempo, *"Tick, tock, tick tock, Tick, tock, tick tock,"* ie 8 pulses for the children to establish a marked pulse, before you then sing, *"Off you go!"*

Published by The Voices Foundation and Alfred Publishing Co
© The Voices Foundation 2014

SET FOUR Distinguishing rhythm and pulse

Class sings one of the songs from this list:

- Goblins are around tonight
- *I like coffee, I like tea*
- *Plainie clappie*
- *Spinning top*

During the following activities which should be spread over a number of days, the song should be periodically changed; the song's tempo and starting pitch should also be varied from time to time; this will help class concentration and 'refresh' the song

- Class sings and simultaneously taps the rhythm [see SET TWO]

- Class sings and simultaneously marks the pulse [see SET THREE]

- Divide the class into two groups: A sings and performs the rhythm; B sings and marks the pulse; in each group, one child performs on a percussion instrument

- As above, but the groups reverse the activities

- As above, but everyone uses the Thinking Voice while performing the rhythm or the pulse

- Face to face in pairs, one child taps the rhythm on their hands while the other marks the steady pulse by tapping the chest

- As above, but roles are reversed

- Two children, each with a different type of percussion instrument, one performs the rhythm while the other marks the pulse

SET FIVE Metre

Teach and secure the song *'Obwisana'* and its game

- Sing the song with these actions to mark the pulse:

  - Class kneeling with legs under, each child taps the floor with hands either side of their knees and then both hands tapping the upper legs to this pattern: **floor** - legs - legs - legs **floor** - legs - legs - legs

  - As above, with the addition of three percussion instruments to play on each 'floor pulse', but only one of the three to continue with the 'legs pulses'

The above activities can be used for:

- Goblins are around tonight
- *I like coffee, I like tea*
- *Spinning top*

- Different actions could be devised to demonstrate the pulse pattern of four, ie **strong** - weak - weak - weak

Listen to the recorded pieces listed under LISTENING

Each piece has a metre of four beats

- Actions from those used for the songs, could also be used to feel the metre of four beats as the children listen

- Background information to the pieces appears in the Listening Material section of this book

LEARNING OUTCOMES

- Children can tap the rhythm of song melody

- Children can mark the pulse as they sing a song

- Children can distinguish between pulse and rhythm and demonstrate this

- Children are aware of the concept of metre

Published by The Voices Foundation and Alfred Publishing Co
© The Voices Foundation 2014

Two weeks

FOCUS

- Listening and thinking
- Concepts: pitch, dynamics, tempo, phrase

TEACHING OBJECTIVES

- To learn that:

  - pitch levels can be compared as being higher or lower

  - dynamic levels can be compared as being louder or quieter

  - tempos [speeds] can be compared as being faster or slower

- To develop the experience of using the Thinking Voice

WHAT IS GOING TO HAPPEN?

- Songs are performed and music heard with changeable pitch, dynamics and tempo
- The Singing Voice, Thinking Voice and actions are used to highlight particular phrases in songs

SONGS

Songs / chant for pitch comparisons

Chest, chest, knee, toe [page 114]

Ding dong, I've got the rhythm [page 116]

I heard, I heard [page 130]

Say, boom, chicka boom [page 147]

Songs / chant for dynamic comparisons

I have lost the cupboard key [page 130]

Oo-a-lay-lay [page 139]

Say, boom, chicka boom [page 147]

Songs / chant for tempo comparisons

Button you must wander [page 112]

I heard, I heard [page 130]

Say, boom, chicka boom [page 147]

HOT SONG

Have you ever, ever? [page 122]

LISTENING

In the Hall of the Mountain King - Grieg [track 81]

GENERAL GUIDANCE

The class already has experience of pitch, dynamics and tempo; now they will be making comparisons within each of those concepts.

The inner Thinking Voice is a crucial skill to making music and the development of musicianship.

The teaching and learning should come out of the songs. For this to happen successfully, the songs should first be very familiar.

Every session should aim for 80% actual making music, 20% for talking and discussion; stay within the medium of music as much as possible.

Published by The Voices Foundation and Alfred Publishing Co

SET ONE Pitch: higher and lower

Chant 'Say, boom, chicka boom'

- Leader and class speak the chant: NO pitch

- First leader imitated by the class, chants on a single pitch; second leader uses a different single pitch; *"Which leader gave us a higher pitch to sing to?"*

Sing 'Chest, chest, knee, toe'

The actions [See Song page] demonstrate the relative pitch levels, so 'head' is the highest pitch and 'toe' the lowest pitch

- Sing with actions

- Perform with Thinking Voice and actions

- With actions, sing the 'head' and 'toe' notes, but use Thinking Voice for the rest

- Leader points to 'chest', class sings the pitch; then points to 'toe', class sings

- As leader points to chest, knee, chest, toe, class sings the relevant word and pitch

- *"Which action gives us the middle pitch?"* [knee]

Sing 'Ding dong, I've got the rhythm'

- Sing with the actions [see Song page]

- With all actions, sing only the words 'Ding dong' and 'Hot dog'; each has the same pair of notes, one higher, one lower in pitch: *"Which words have the lower pitch?"* [dong and dog]

Sing 'I heard, I heard'

- 'I heard' and 'To-day' each have the same pair of notes, one higher and one lower: *"Which word or syllable has the higher pitch?"* [heard and day]

SET TWO Dynamics: louder and quieter

Chant 'Say, boom, chicka boom'

- Leader and class speak the chant quietly

- Leader and class speak the chant more loudly

- Leader speaks each phrase at a slightly different volume; class imitates

Sing 'The Owlet'

Class is divided into two equal groups

Make sure the children stay with the Singing Voice and don't engage the Shouting Voice!

Group A sings the lead phrases alternately quiet and loud; group B echo each phrase with the same dynamic

Group B sings the lead phrases alternately loud and quiet; group A sing the opposite dynamic

Play the game as outlined on the Song page

SET THREE Tempo: faster and slower

Chant 'Say, boom, chicka boom'

- The leader selects a moderate speed that the class imitate in its response

- The leader now selects, without announcement, either a faster or slower speed; again the class must match in its response: which performance was faster?

Sing 'Button you must wander'

- You tap on an instrument a steady pulse for four counts before the class sing the song to the set tempo; ask if the tempo was maintained accurately

- Repeat the above, but to new tempo; ask if the second tempo was faster or slower than the first

Sing 'I heard, I heard'

- The leader sets a tempo that is taken up by the class in its responses

- A new leader sets a new tempo; afterwards the leader must say whether the class accurately imitated the tempo and whether it was faster or slower than the first leader; does the class agree?

SET FOUR Listening to the three comparatives

Play the 'In the Hall of the Mountain King'

- Ask the class to listen out for the pitch, dynamics and tempo, and to say afterwards what they particularly noticed

- Children have the ability to compare differences in pitch, dynamics and tempo

- Children have the ability to control pitch, dynamics and tempo

- Children can identify changes of pitch, dynamics and tempo within a piece of music

Published by The Voices Foundation and Alfred Publishing Co
© The Voices Foundation 2014

Three weeks

FOCUS

- Performing: playing
- Concept: rhythm

TEACHING OBJECTIVES

- To learn to play song rhythms on untuned percussion
- To understand the basic principles of simple time rhythm
- To learn to use spoken rhythm names for simple time

WHAT IS GOING TO HAPPEN?

- Experiencing song and chant rhythms through speaking and tapping
- Playing chant and song rhythms on percussion
- Performing the pattern of two notes within one pulse
- Using the performing rhythm names ta and teh-teh

SONGS

Can you tap this rhythm? [page 113]

Double, double [page 117]

Here sits a fat cat [page 124] *

Plainie clappie [page 142]

Rain, rain, go away [page 144] *

Starlight, star bright [page 150]

Suo gân [page 152]

HOT SONG

Bubblegum, bubblegum [page 111]

LISTENING

Percussion - Britten [track 82]

YouTube: The Young Person's Guide to the Orchestra - Britten, YouTube Symphony Orchestra 2011

GENERAL GUIDANCE

So far, the rhythms of most songs the children have learned contain only a limited number of sounds of different duration. Hence, there are a limited number of patterns and these occur repeatedly in the songs. Here we identify two elements of these patterns and give them each a speaking name: **ta** and **teh-teh**

The teaching principle is **'sound before symbol'**. In other words, before children see and use music notation, they should first experience the elements of rhythm through song and chant and then aurally identify them. This approach will then lead to reading and writing and ensure that music notation is a natural consequence, is 'real', and not 'abstract' or mere theory. All this has much in common with other areas of learning, such as language.

Published by The Voices Foundation and Alfred Publishing Co
© The Voices Foundation 2014

SET ONE Rhythm in songs and chant

Teach / chant and work with titles from this list:

- Double, double
- *Here sits a fat cat* *
- Plainie clappie
- *Rain, rain, go away* *
- *Starlight, star bright*
- Suo gân

- Select a song / chant and class performs it

- Class performs and simultaneously taps the rhythm

- Repeat, but using the Speaking Voice and tapping

- Repeat, but using the Thinking Voice and tapping

Select a first phrase only from one of the titles in the above list

For the following, you will need to have several untuned percussion instruments to hand

- Class sings/chants the phrase and simultaneously taps it

- Repeat, but using the Thinking Voice and tapping

- Several instruments perform the phrase

- Work with other first phrases in other known songs

SET TWO Introducing ta and teh-teh

- On a hand held instrument you tap a steady and regular sound at a moderate speed [tempo] and simultaneously say with each tap, 'ta'; do this for 8 counts

- Repeat the above, with the class tapping and speaking 'ta'

- With the children marking the steady and regular pulse with the 'heartbeat' tap on the chest, you tap two equal length sounds to each pulse on the instrument and speak 'teh-teh'; do this for about 8 counts

- Repeat the above, with the class providing a tapped 'heartbeat' pulse and speaking 'teh-teh' for each pulse

- With a steady 'heartbeat' pulse from the class, you tap on an instrument, one sound to each pulse and speak 'ta'; the children join in; at some point and without prior warning you change to two equal length sounds to each pulse and speak 'teh-teh'; the class change to **speaking** 'teh-teh' as well; eventually you revert back to 'ta' and the class also

- As above, but the leader uses the Thinking Voice while the class provides the spoken rhythm names

Published by The Voices Foundation and Alfred Publishing Co
© The Voices Foundation 2014

SET THREE Speaking rhythm phrases with rhythm names

Work with phrases from this list:

- Double, double
- *Here sits a fat cat* *
- Plainie clappie
- *Rain, rain, go away* *
- *Starlight, star bright*
- Suo gân

The following are the rhythm names of phrase 1 in these songs / chants:

Here	sits a	fat	cat
ta	**teh-teh**	**ta**	**ta**
Rain,	rain,	go a -	way
ta	**ta**	**teh-teh**	**ta**
Star	light,	star	bright,
ta	**ta**	**ta**	**ta**
first	star I've	seen to -	night
ta	**teh-teh**	**teh-teh**	**ta**

Plain -	ie	clap -	pie
ta	**ta**	**ta**	**ta**
roll-ing	pin to	back -	ie
teh-teh	**teh-teh**	**ta**	**ta**
Su - o	gân,	do not	weep
teh-teh	**ta**	**teh-teh**	**ta**
Dou-ble,	dou-ble,	this,	this
teh - teh	**teh-teh**	**ta**	**ta**

To a steady pulse, you speak the words, then speak the rhythm names; the children repeat

SET FOUR Listening to the percussion

Listen to the percussion excerpt from Benjamin Britten's 'The Young Person's Guide to the Orchestra' on CD 2, alternatively there is an excellent YouTube video recording of the whole piece by YouTube Symphony Orchestra. Slide the play button along until you reach the percussion section and the finale.

- Listen to the changing dynamics
- Which instruments are being used? Stringed instruments accompany throughout. Display the list, so that over several hearings, the class can associate the sounds of the instruments with the relevant names:

  1. Three timpani drums
  2. Bass drum and cymbals
  3. Tambourine
  4. Triangle
  5. Side [snare] drum
  6. Woodblock
  7. Xylophone
  8. Castanets
  9. Gong
  10. Whip
  11. 'All together'
  12. The 'fade' instrument?

Pictures of these instruments are available through Google: "Images of percussion instruments"

LEARNING OUTCOMES

- Children can perform the rhythms of known songs
- Children can perform one sound per pulse and two sounds of equal duration per pulse
- Children can use the rhythm names, ta and teh-teh, when speaking rhythm phrases from known songs
- Children can listen to a range of percussion instruments in a piece of music by Benjamin Britten and will know their names

Published by The Voices Foundation and Alfred Publishing Co
© The Voices Foundation 2014

FOCUS

- Singing Development
- Concepts: pitch, timbre

TEACHING OBJECTIVES

- To raise a general awareness of Singing Voice sound qualities
- To develop an understanding of and skills to influence the singing of vowels
- To listen to pitch changes in song phrases and to show the melodic line through hand movement
- To listen to a specific interval [pitch distance] between two levels of pitch in song melody
- To learn to recognise the interval with singing-names [solfa]: **soh** for the higher pitch, **me** for the lower pitch
- To learn to associate **soh** and **me** with their supporting handsigns

WHAT IS GOING TO HAPPEN?

- Singing with awareness of features that influence the 'tone-colour' of the Singing Voice
- Listening to the 'tone-colour' of others in recorded music
- Children sense the pitch movements in song melody and show this using hand movement.
- Chime bars are used to illustrate pitch changes
- Song phrases using the **soh - me** interval are sung to singing names supported by related handsigns
- 'Unknown' pitch phrases using **soh** and **me** are sung to singing names supported by related handsigns

SONGS

Singing Development Songs: tone 1

Heno, heno, hen blant bach [page 123]

Salani [page 146]

For awareness of pitch change

Bells in the steeple [page 109]

High, low, chickalow [page 126]

We can sing high [page 153]

For identifying soh and me

Ev'ryone, good morning [page 119]

Here I come [page 124]

I like coffee, I like tea [page 131]

I, I, me oh my [page 131] *

Rain, rain, go away [page 144] *

HOT SONG

Bounce high, bounce low [page 109]

LISTENING

'O Euchari' – St. Hildegard [track 83]

The Swan – Saint-Saëns [track 77]

YouTube: 'Hwb – Heno, heno, hen blant bach [20/10/12]'

Published by The Voices Foundation and Alfred Publishing Co
© The Voices Foundation 2014

There are no secrets about the Singing Voice; we can all have access to how it works. If we have the opportunities to develop the skills and understanding, the mystique and fears of using the Singing Voice are lifted. Each Singing Voice has organic possibilities and through guidance and teaching, singers will develop skills and understanding about how to control the sound they produce; they will be able to make choices.

Pitch cannot be seen, it is aurally sensed and the brain interprets those sense impressions as a sound that is relatively higher or lower when placed alongside another pitched sound.

Actions and visual symbols can provide an illustration of the movement of pitch in a melody, but to have any useful meaning they need to have a resonance with the aural senses and memory. The Singing Voice does not have a system of keys or mechanisms like instruments, such as pianos and flutes; the aural brain and its memory is the only way of determining the pitch that the Singing Voice will make. To read and write music notation with specific pitch, the reader needs a system that, with practice, will enable this. For this to happen, the system known as Sol-fa is advocated as part of the development of reading music notation with the Singing Voice. Eventually, Sol-fa will make possible the reading of pitch on a five-line stave [staff].

Sol-fa gives us singing names for vocal pitch, such as, doh, ray, me, fah, soh, lah. This Unit explores the relationship of soh with me. They have a specific interval connection that we will find in some of the children's songs.

Supporting handsigns for the singing names are important for reinforcing the memory of the soh - me interval.

SET ONE Singing Development: tone or sound quality

It may seem odd to use a language unfamiliar to the children, but this will put exploring the tone colours onto a 'neutral base' and perhaps negate some prejudices about accent, dialect and 'sounding posh'!

Sing 'Salani'

- Listen carefully to the sounds of the words in the recording on CD-2

Consider the AH sound of the first syllable

- Warm-up exercises. Ask the children to:
  - give you a drop-jaw look of surprise [You just offered them something nice?]
  - give you a slow yawn
  - balance a Smartie [or similar sweet] on the tongue
  - pretend to put on lip-balm
- Then, together with bright eyes, to try all those things simultaneously as they sing phrases 1 and 2 to the one vowel 'AH'

Consider the EE sound of the third syllable

- Warm-up exercises. Ask the children to:
  - feel the back of the lower front teeth with the tip of the tongue
  - lower the jaw and place one finger resting sideways between the teeth
  - pretend to put on lip-stick – including the boys!
- Then, together with bright eyes, to try all those things simultaneously as they sing phrases 1 and 2 to the one vowel 'EE'
- Sing the whole song attempting to focus on these vowels when they arise.

SET TWO A song in Welsh

Watch the YouTube video of 'Heno, heno, hen blant bach'

- Listen carefully as the Welsh sounds are taught by Welsh speakers
- Teach the song

Published by The Voices Foundation and Alfred Publishing Co
© The Voices Foundation 2014

SET THREE The sound qualities of voice and cello

Listen to 'O Euchari'

- What do the children notice about the tone-colour of the singing sound? What words help to describe the sound qualities? Shades of colour? A warm brown?

Listen to 'The Swan'

The sound of the cello is often thought of as resembling the human Singing Voice

- Using the same sort of questions as for 'O Euchari', how do the children describe the sound quality of the cello in this piece?

SET FOUR Demonstrating the movement of pitch

Sing 'High, low, chickalow'

The hand movements of the clapping game and the pitch movement coincide

Sing 'We can sing high'

- The class 'draws' in the air with their index fingers, the pitch movement as they sing

- As a leader and the class sing, the leader demonstrates the 'drawing'

Sing 'Bells in the steeple'

- Class sings phrase 1 only

- Tell the class that there are only three different levels of pitch; for the lowest pitch the class touch their shoulders; for the 'middle' pitch of the three, they touch ears; for the highest they touch the top of their head; singing the phrase to 'nah' for each note and starting with the 'shoulder' pitch, the children demonstrate the pitch movement as they sing; the phrase follows this pattern:

Head   ● ● ●

Ears   ● ● ●   ●

Shoulders   ● ● ●

Three chime bars with appropriate beaters play phrase 1, where -

F, the longest of the three bars, plays the 'shoulder' notes
A, the slightly shorter bar, plays the 'ear' notes
C, the shortest bar, plays the 'head' notes

SET FIVE Introducing soh and me

Sing songs from this list:

- Ev'ryone, good morning

- Here I come

- I like coffee, I like tea

- *I, I, me oh my* *

These songs have melodies with only two pitches

The pitch interval [vertical difference] between the two notes is the same in each song

The singing names remain constant too, **soh** [the higher pitch] and **me** [the lower pitch]

- After the singing of a song, you sing:
  *"Higher sound **soh**, lower sound **me**"* to the pitches just used; class copies

- After the singing of a song, you sing, **soh me** to the pitches just used with these supporting handsigns; class copies

soh [mouth level]   **me** [chest-top level]

- Sing the phrase, 'I, I, me oh my', followed immediately by the singing names to the same rhythm and with supporting handsigns:

soh - me - soh - soh - me

the class copies

- Use the above process for:

'Ev'ryone, good morning'   = **s-s-m-m-s-m**

'I like coffee, I like tea'   = **s-s-m-m-s-s-m**

'Here I come. Where from?'   = **s-s-m-s-m**

LEARNING OUTCOMES

- Children are aware that sound quality is a feature of performing

- Children know that vocal tone can be changed

- Children can aurally identify and demonstrate the movement of pitch in song phrases

- Children have learned that the **soh - me** interval is a common feature of melody

Published by The Voices Foundation and Alfred Publishing Co
© The Voices Foundation 2014

FOCUS

- Singing Development
- Listening and thinking
- Concept: rhythm

LISTENING

- Nun, Gimel, Hei, Shin [track 84]
- Oliver Cromwell [track 85]
- The Arrival of the Queen of Sheba [track 86]

TEACHING OBJECTIVES

- To increase the accuracy and stability of pitch when singing: 'singing in tune'
- To listen to recorded pieces with purpose
- To identify a song from only its performed rhythm
- To develop early skills in improvising

GENERAL GUIDANCE

Singing 'in tune' is an aspect that singers and listeners will feel is important. Singing 'out of tune' can be the result of aural inexperience, poor breath support, tiredness, anxiety or distraction. On the aural and technical aspects, singers will be helped enormously by this programme through the use of sol-fa, the teaching ideas and the regularity of singing.

Schools strive to give their pupils quality materials and quality experiences. The quality of sound reproduction for the recorded music and YouTube examples is important for children. If the sound reproduction is impaired, it is likely that the reception to the listening material will be less enthusiastic.

The aural memory and the Thinking Voice are central to identifying a song from just its performed rhythm. The same two features also play a key role in the skills of improvising.

Improvising has many levels of activity. Essentially it is about making spontaneous or late decisions about what will happen while performing. The performer or performers make choices about the structural elements, such as rhythm, pitch and dynamics.

WHAT IS GOING TO HAPPEN?

- Children are taught how to focus the singing pitch through listening and using breath support
- Hearing recorded music with questions to focus the listening
- From a pool of known song titles, a song is identified by its rhythm only
- Known rhythm phrases form the basis of opportunities for choice and spontaneity

SONGS

Singing Development Songs: singing in tune 1

Bells in the steeple [page 109]

Michael row the boat ashore [page 135]

Spinning top [page 149]

Song/chant list:

Double, double [page 117]

Ev'ryone, good morning [page 119]

Plainie clappie [page 142]

Rain, rain, go away [page 144] *

Spinning top [page 149]

Starlight, star bright [page 150]

Suo gân [page 152]

HOT SONG

Published by The Voices Foundation and Alfred Publishing Co

SET ONE Singing 'in tune'

IMPORTANT! Tackle this when the time feels right: it requires mental and physical focus, commitment and energy!

A pitched instrument is required, preferably one that can sustain a sound for a brief period, such as a keyboard, <u>large</u> pitch percussion, stringed instrument [guitar, violin], treble/tenor recorder; <u>if at all possible, the instrument should be capable of giving notes that equate to the children's singing pitch - glockenspiels do not do this.</u>

Select one of the three songs listed in SONGS; it should be confidently known

- The starting pitch for each song will be note F on the instrument

- The class stands with a supportive posture

- The note F is given from an instrument and quietly hummed

- The song is quietly sung using F as the starting note

- At the end of the melody the instrument immediately plays the F again:

  "Was the pitch of the singing and instrument exactly the same?"

Tips for staying in tune:

- Supportive posture [Unit 3]

- Supportive breath from low down: when the pitch rises we need to 'tighten our belts' [Unit 6]

- Think slightly above the note

- Sing more quietly

- Listen 'hard' to yourself and others, ie focus and concentrate

SET TWO Focused listening to recorded music

This piece, sung by children in Hebrew, celebrates the Jewish festival of Hanukkah

  By marking the 'heartbeat' pulse, can the class hear the changes of speed [tempo]?

  Did they hear the soloist?

  How did the music end?

This is a Suffolk nursery rhyme

  Who is Oliver? What happens to him?

  Mark the pulse to find the tempo

  How many voices are singing?

Background notes are given for each recorded music track in the Listening Material pages

  Give no title, but ask the class whose arrival they feel is being announced by the music

SET THREE Recognising a song from its rhythm only

Select two known songs/chant from the SONGS list

- Class sings/speaks the two songs / chant

- Using the Thinking Voice, the class 'silently' sings/speaks the same songs/chant while tapping the rhythm

- Without prior announcement, you tap on a percussion instrument the rhythm of one of the two items; when complete, and after *"Off you go!"*, the class sings/chants their collective 'answer'

- As above, but an individual is selected to sing/chant their answer

- Select another pair of songs/chant and follow the above process

- Invite a child to be the leader in selecting the songs/chant

- Invite a child to be the leader and play the rhythm to be identified

SET FOUR Choosing a rhythm answer

Class sings these three songs:

- Ev'ryone, good morning
- Plainie clappie
- Suo gân

For the words 'Ev'ryone good morning', class taps and speaks:

teh-teh teh-teh ta ta

For the words 'Plainie clappie', class taps and speaks:

ta ta ta ta

For the words 'Suo gân, do not weep', class taps and speaks:

teh-teh ta teh-teh ta

- The three rhythms are displayed as rhythm names

- Without prior announcement, you tap and speak the rhythm names of one of the above rhythms; the children each select one of the other two rhythms and after a spoken *"Off you go!"* simultaneously tap and speak their chosen rhythm names

- As above with a different rhythm, but the class follows on immediately ie no *"Off you go!"*

- As above, but with child leader using a percussion instrument

- As above, but with two individuals, each using a different percussion instrument: a 'question phrase' followed by an 'answer phrase'

- As above, but the rhythm names are not seen

- As above, but the rhythm names are 'spoken' by the Thinking Voice

Published by The Voices Foundation and Alfred Publishing Co
© The Voices Foundation 2014

FOCUS

- Performing: playing pitch [tuned] percussion

TEACHING OBJECTIVES

- To acquire basic co-ordination and playing skills on pitch percussion, eg xylophone, glockenspiel, chime bars
- To play several known song phrases
- To improvise melodic phrases on pitch percussion

WHAT IS GOING TO HAPPEN?

- Considering fundamentals of instrument and beater [mallet] suitability, logistics and posture
- Addressing important beater-holding and wrist action issues
- Playing by ear known song phrases using the **soh - me** singing interval
- Improvising new instrumental phrases

SONGS

Doggie, doggie [page 116] *

Ev'ryone, good morning [page 119]

Fire! Fire! [page 120]

Here I come [page 124]

I, I, me oh my [page 131] *

Rain, rain, go away [page 144] *

HOT SONG

I can take my tea [page 129]

LISTENING

YouTube: 'How to properly hold a mallet'; 'How to properly strike a xylophone' [Mahalo.com]

Toccata - Pitfield [track 87]

GENERAL GUIDANCE

All instruments have accepted conventions for playing which, if used, lead to improved technical skill for the player. Tuned [pitch] percussion, such as the xylophone, are normally available to schools and there are versions of these instruments played in the concert hall or in communities throughout the world. In this programme, children are introduced to some of the basic skills of playing. YouTube videos and live professional demonstration can help to impart those skills. The mallet in the suggested YouTube example is also a stick or beater.

Whether the tuned [pitch] percussion instruments have bars that are made of wood or metal, it is best if they can sound pitch at the children's singing pitch; larger instruments, usually designated as alto or tenor, will do this while smaller instruments will sound well above the children's Singing Voices.

Beaters [USA: mallets] come in various sizes and handle lengths; the head can be made of different materials - wood, rubber, cord, felt. Harder heads generally produce a 'harder' and naturally louder sound and conversely heads that are made of felt or soft rubber a mellow and quieter sound.

Ideally there should be a range of beaters available and in numbers that allow for two of a kind to be used with each instrument.

Addressing the instrument with a correct posture is important as it will allow for the correct handling of the beaters; the relative heights of player and instrument should also be addressed - see the YouTube Mahalo.com series 'How to play xylophone for beginners' Part I Basics

SET ONE Playing pitch percussion

See GENERAL GUIDANCE concerning pitch of tuned percussion

See the advice about beaters under GENERAL GUIDANCE

Holding the beaters in an approved way will assist skill development

The player needs to play with a beater [mallet] in each hand and to use them in combination as well as separately

In the following example, the beaters are used alternately

Sing the greeting 'Ev'ryone, good morning'

- Sing phrase 1 to the singing names with supporting handsigns:

soh soh me me soh me [s s m m s m]

- With the class kneeling in a circle or seated in several circles on chairs, let:

left leg = me   right leg = soh

- Starting with right hand the children tap alternate hands while singing to the singing names thus:

Singing names	s	s	m	m	s	m
Hand	R	L	R	L	R	L

Watch the YouTube Mahalo.com series 'How to play xylophone for beginners' Part 1 Basics

Working with beaters

- Let each child hold a beater in **each** hand; if there are insufficient beaters use two long pencils or similar

- Recall the videos and how to hold the beaters [mallets]

- All sing the song phrase to singing names and perform with beaters on the legs as above

'Tuning' the singing voice to the pitch percussion instrument eg xylophone

C   D   E   F   G   A   B   C

- G and E bars are played consecutively; class sings **soh - me**; class 'tunes' the 'legs', their xylophone bars, playing and <u>singing the instrument names</u>:

E = left leg   G = right leg

- Starting on G, children sing the song phrase ['Ev'ryone good morning'] to instrument names and play their 'instrument' thus:

Instrument names	G	G	E	E	G	E
Hand	R	L	R	L	R	L

- Children play the song melody on available pitch percussion as the class listens or supports, eg quietly singing the instrument names

- Concert performance: instruments play the melody; children sing the song; both instruments and voices perform

SET TWO Playing song phrases

All the first phrases of the songs in the SONGS list start on **soh** and use **soh** and **me**

All the first phrases can be played on pitch percussion using **G soh** and **E me**; however as alternatives, there are **F soh** and **D me** and **C soh** and **A me**

Encourage the use of both beaters playing alternately

Select a first phrase from a known song in the list and use the process of SET ONE

Later, give individuals opportunities to spontaneously select and play one of these phrases without the SET ONE process, ie play by ear

Published by The Voices Foundation and Alfred Publishing Co

SET THREE Improvising

Ideally, have two pitch percussion instruments to hand, each with a pair of beaters

The players have G and E available to use

- Using the Thinking Voice, a leader taps on an untuned instrument a rhythm phrase from one of the songs in the SONGS list without identifying which; the player repeats the rhythm with improvised pitch

- Two instruments and two players: a song phrase rhythm is tapped by a leader; child A repeats adding a spontaneous pitch element; child B copies

- Two instruments and two players: a song phrase rhythm is tapped; child A improvises a pitch element; child B uses the same rhythm but with a different pitch to A

Improvising a piece for two pitch percussion instruments

- The players have the five consecutive notes D E F G A to use

- They are given the rhythm:

  teh-teh teh-teh ta ta ['Ev'ryone good morning']

  Each child uses the same rhythm phrase, but can use a few, some or all of the given pitches to improvise the pitch element

- The improvised piece is to consist of four phrases in the following sequence: child 1 - child 2 - child 1 - child 2

- The tempo should be stable throughout

SET FOUR Listen to the xylophone

The word 'toccata', like many terms used in music, comes from the Italian, and means 'to touch'; it has come to be associated with music that is showy and tests the technical skills of the performer

Can the children imagine playing this piece on the xylophone?

LEARNING OUTCOMES

- Children have acquired some basic skills when playing tuned [pitch] percussion instruments

- Children are able to play song phrases on tuned [pitch] percussion

- Children can improvise on tuned [pitch] percussions, a pitch element to a given rhythm

Published by The Voices Foundation and Alfred Publishing Co
© The Voices Foundation 2014

Two weeks

FOCUS

- Singing Development

- Performing: singing, playing instruments

- Concepts: pitch, rhythm, pulse, phrase, tempo, dynamics, timbre

TEACHING OBJECTIVES

- To reinforce and assess the skills, knowledge and understanding in the areas of singing development, performing, listening and concepts, acquired during the teaching of Units 1 - 12

WHAT IS GOING TO HAPPEN?

- Activities are used that allow the class and individuals to demonstrate their skills, knowledge and understanding

SONGS

Using songs as listed under the different Teaching Ideas headings

HOT SONG

LISTENING

O Polichinelo [Punch] - Villa-Lobos [track 88]

A Pobrezinha [Rag Doll] - Villa-Lobos [track 89]

GENERAL GUIDANCE

This Revision Unit provides an opportunity for the children to revisit and reinforce some of the skills and knowledge they have encountered so far. It is also a moment when the teacher can assess how well these developments have been assimilated by the children. It is time to take stock before moving on.

The teacher is given options of repertoire to use. Select songs with which the children are really familiar.

The assessment criteria head each section in the form of questions to the teacher.

IMPORTANT! The teacher can choose to use all the activities or as few as is necessary to demonstrate the children's competences and is helpful revision for the children.

Published by The Voices Foundation and Alfred Publishing Co
© The Voices Foundation 2014

Singing Voice and Thinking Voice

Assessing:

Has the Singing Voice been 'found'?

Do they demonstrate a supportive posture when standing?

Do the children breathe easily and sing with one breath per phrase?

Can the sound be described as pleasing to the ear?

Does the singing sound in tune?

Can children use the Thinking Voice when working with song phrases and rhythms?

Select one of the these songs known to the class:

- Michael row the boat ashore [page 135] [D : D] +

- Summer goodbye [page 151] [A : F] +

- Starlight, star bright [page 150] [G : C] +

- Class stands to sing the song with 'best voices'

- Class sits to sing the song showing you a 'good' sitting posture

- Class sings demonstrating ease when taking a breath for each new phrase

- A starting pitch is taken from a suitable instrument; after singing the last note, the end pitch is played; do the final singing pitch and the instrument match? See the suggested starting and finishing instruments notes against the titles [+]

- Mirrors: A leader sings the first phrase to a child who must imitate at the leader's pitch

- Relay: First child sings phrase 1, second child phrase 2, and so on; each succeeding child takes up the pitch established by the first child

- While marking the pulse, the class alternates between the Singing Voice and Thinking Voice for successive phrases

Instrument playing

Assessing:

Are percussion instruments known by their proper names?

Are instruments respected and cared for?

Does the posture and holding of certain instruments help to facilitate playing?

Can children play song rhythms on untuned percussion instruments?

Do the relative heights of player and a tuned percussion instrument facilitate the use of beaters [mallets]?

Can children play tuned percussion using two beaters?

Can children play a simple song phrase?

Several children are asked to bring forward several untuned and tuned percussion instruments named by the teacher

- They report on the conditions in which they had found the instruments

- Do they bring forward the asked-for instruments?

Select a song from:

- Bounce high, bounce low [page 109]

- Here sits a fat cat * [page 124]

- High, low, chickalow [page 126]

- Plainie clappie [page 142]

- Class sings the song

- Class taps the rhythm and uses the Thinking Voice

- Child names an untuned percussion instrument, collects it and performs the rhythm of the song while using their Thinking Voice

- Two children, each with a different untuned instrument, play alternate phrases

Select a song from:

- Doggie, doggie * [page 116]

- Ev'ryone, good morning [page 119]

- Fire! Fire! [page 120]

- I, I, me oh my * [page 131]

- Rain, rain, go away * [page 144]

At the end of the song, class sings: **G soh**, **E me** at their respective pitches

One or several tuned percussion instruments play bars labelled **G** then **E**

Class sings the song marking the pulse and accompanied by the player[s], performing with the steady pulse alternating between **G** and **E**

An individual elects to play phrase 1 of the song's melody

Listening to recorded music

Are children able to listen with a given focus and to give comments afterwards?

Is the class familiar with 'Punch and Judy'?

Punch is up to wild mischief! But what?

What is a rag doll? What does the music tell us about Rag Doll?

Concepts: rhythm and pulse

Can children tap song rhythms?

Can children mark the pulse as they sing?

Can children demonstrate the difference between rhythm and pulse?

Can children perform song rhythms using rhythm names **[ta + teh-teh]**?

Are children aware of the concept of metre?

Double, double [page 117]
[teh-teh teh-teh ta ta]

I, I, me oh my * [page 131]
[ta ta teh-teh ta]

Rain, rain, go away * [page 144]
[ta ta teh-teh ta]

Spinning top [page 149]
[teh-teh teh-teh teh-teh ta]

Starlight, star bright [page 150]
[ta ta ta ta]

Suo gân [page 152]
[teh-teh ta teh-teh ta]

Class sings and taps the rhythm

Class sings and marks the pulse

As two groups, one performs the rhythm as the other marks the pulse, all using the Thinking Voice; the melody is repeated, but the groups swap activities

The rhythm of phrase 1 is tapped and the rhythm names 'spoken' in the Thinking Voice

Phrase one is repeated, but the rhythm names are spoken aloud

Facing a partner, class sings and marks the repetitive four metre pulse pattern, thus: **clap own hands x 1 - slap partner's hands x 3**

Published by The Voices Foundation and Alfred Publishing Co

Concept: pitch

Are children able to show through action the changes in pitch as they occur in a melody?

Are children able to compare two consecutive performances or notes as being relatively higher or lower?

*Can children sing song phrases to the sol-fa singing names, **soh** and **me**, with supporting handsigns?*

Class sings 'Michael row the boat ashore' [page 135]

- As they sing phrases 1 and 2, children show the vertical movement of the pitch with one hand in front

- A leader sings phrase1, the rest join in at the leaders pitch for phrase 2; a second leader is asked to start at a different pitch and the class matches it for phrase 2; was the second time higher or lower in pitch? [Teacher: it might be the same pitch! Do the class recognise that?]

Class performs 'I like coffee, I like tea' [page 131]

- Sing phrase1 only

- Sing to the singing names **soh** and **me** with supporting handsigns
  [s - s - m - m - s - s - m]

- Ask individuals to sing the phrase to singing names

- As two class groups, A sings just the 'soh's, the other just the 'me's

Concept: phrase

Can children imitate a sung phrase and a tapped rhythm phrase?

Can children demonstrate with 'rainbow' actions the duration of a phrase when singing songs?

Concepts: tempo; dynamics; timbre

Can children identify the tempo of music through marking the speed of the pulse?

Can children compare the tempo of two performances as being relatively slower or faster?

Are children able to sing or play with different dynamics?

Can they identify two consecutive performances as being relatively quieter or louder?

Can children put names to known voices and instruments performing unseen?

Are children able to use language to describe the different sounds made by voices and instruments?

Class sings 'Here I come' [page 124]

- The leader sings the calls and sets a certain tempo which the class in their responses must follow, all must mark the pulse

- As above, but a second leader deliberately sets a different tempo; compare the tempos as being faster or slower

- The leader sings the calls at a certain dynamic which the class must follow

- As above, but the new leader chooses a different dynamic; compare the dynamics as being quieter or louder

- Two or three untuned instruments are placed out of sight, but within audible distance; two or three children are sent to the instruments; one child only chooses an instrument and sings and plays the rhythm of the calls; the class sings the responses. Can the class identify who sang and name the instrument used? Can they describe the distinctive features of the voice and instrument timbres?

LEARNING OUTCOMES

- Children have reinforced their skills, understanding and knowledge covered in Units 1 - 12

Two weeks

Published by The Voices Foundation and Alfred Publishing Co
© The Voices Foundation 2014

FOCUS

- Concepts: phrase, tempo

TEACHING OBJECTIVES

- To compare the phrases of a known song as being the same or different

- To show that phrases in the same song can be of different lengths

- To show that tempo [speed] is important to the character of the song

WHAT IS GOING TO HAPPEN?

- The phrases of a song will be identified and compared as being the same or different

- The number of beats in each phrase of a song will be identified and the resulting lengths compared

- A song is performed to various tempos [tempi] and its most suitable speed identified

- Children listen to pieces of recorded music:
  - to identify and compare the phrases
  - with contrasting tempos

SONGS

Bells in the steeple [page 109]

Fire! Fire! [page 120]

Goblins are around tonight [page 121]

John the blacksmith [page 134]

Old King Glory [page 137]

Spinning top [page 149]

Starlight, star bright [page 150]

HOT SONG

Hi! My name's Joe [page 125]

LISTENING

'The Green Man' – Anon [track 92]

Bydło – Mussorgsky [track 90]

Flight of the Bumblebee – Rimsky-Korsakov [track 91]

GENERAL GUIDANCE

Phrases are the basic building blocks in a piece of music. Music is often memorable because it appeals to the aural senses, much like a building might appeal to the visual senses. The appeal in music is often because the phrase structure satisfies our desire for proportion and balance. Repetition is an important aspect in aural structure for most listeners, but then phrases with different music content are normally needed for structural balance. In songs the melodic phrases are given life through a mix of rhythm and pitch, but that mix has its origins in the lyrics of the song. The songwriter is challenged to set the words to musical phrases that are sympathetic to the words and enrich their meaning and message.

A phrase length is sometimes a matter of interpretation and opinion and these differences can often have equal validity. Some of the songs in the Song pages are given phrase marks. For songs without phrase marks, then the punctuation in the lyrics will be helpful.

Tempo is an important feature in expressiveness. Performers strive to find the 'right tempo' for a piece of music. Slight differences in speed can make large differences to an overall effect.

SET ONE Phrases - same or different?

Sing / teach 'John the blacksmith'

This song has a melody of two phrases, each with identical rhythm and pitch

- Class divided into two groups, sings one phrase each

- Using their Thinking Voices, the groups tap the rhythm of their phrase

- The groups hum the melody of their phrases

- Ask the children to compare the music of the two phrases [same]

Sing 'Fire! Fire!'

This song has two phrases, each being rhythmically different

- Class divided into two groups, sing one phrase each

- Using their Thinking Voices, the groups tap the rhythm of their phrase

- Ask the children whether the rhythms were the same or different [different]

Sing / teach 'Old King Glory'

This songs has three phrases, each is different

- Class divided into three groups, sing one phrase each

- The groups each sing their phrase to 'nah'

- Ask the children to compare the phrases as being same or different [different]

SET TWO Phrases - repeated phrases

Sing 'Spinning top'

This song has four phrases where phrases 1 and 2 are repeated as phrases 3 and 4

- Class sings the song demonstrating the four phrase lengths with 'rainbow' arcs - see Unit 6

- Class sings phrases 1 and 3, but uses the Thinking Voice for phrases 2 and 4: What do they notice about the <u>melody</u> of phrases 1 and 3? [same]

- Class uses the Thinking Voice for phrases 1 and 3, but sings phrases 2 and 4: What do they notice about the <u>melody</u> of phrases 2 and 4? [same]

- Ask the children to compare phrases 1 and 2 as being same or different [different]

SET THREE Phrases - different phrase lengths

Sing 'Starlight, star bright'

A song's phrases are not always the same length

- Class sings the song as three phrases according to the phrase marks on the Song page; the teacher shows the 'rainbow' arcs; the class repeats the song adding the 'rainbow' arcs too

- Class sings phrase 1 only, marking the pulse with a gentle tap and counting the number of beats in their heads: "How many beats for phrase 1?" [four]

- As above for phrases 2 [four] and 3 [eight]

SET FOUR Identify the phrases

Sing the songs 'Goblins are around tonight' and 'Bells in the steeple'

- Using the teaching ideas in Sets One and Two, can the children help you to identify the phrases and compare them as same or different?

SET FIVE Listen to The Green Man

The English Dancing Master first appeared as a collection of dance tunes and dance instructions in 1651. The Green Man is the name of a dance from this collection compiled by John Playford.

Dance at this time had a sequence of movements that would correlate with the phrases of the tune. So the phrase beginning, its rhythm and ending are all very pronounced.

- Ask the class to close eyes and listen; on hearing what they feel is a new phrase, they raise a hand for a moment and then lower

- On a repeat listen, they have a pencil and paper and make a mark for each new phrase; at the end they compare with a partner the total number for the piece [8]

- What is the phrase length? Who can count the number of beats there are to each phrase? Suggest they should mark the pulse and count. [8 per phrase]

SET SIX Which tempo is best?

Which tempo does the class feels is the most appropriate for the following songs?

Fire! Fire!

Goblins are round tonight

Starlight, star bright

The leader sets the tempo with four percussion instrument pulse taps and singing in time the starting pitch with *"Off you go!"*

Try different tempos for repeat performances

Ask the class to consider the lyrics and what they might suggest

As a result try a tempo that reflects the broad agreement

SET SEVEN Listening to recorded music

- Compare the tempos of 'Bydło' and 'Flight of the Bumblebee'

For the background information, see the Listening Material pages

- How important do the children consider the tempo is in expressing the character of each piece?

LEARNING OUTCOMES

- Children can identify and compare the phrases in a song melody as being the same, different or repeated

- Children can identify the phrase length by counting the number of beats [pulses]

- Children are aware that phrase lengths in a melody may not always be the same

- Children will be aware that tempo is an important element in musical expression

Published by The Voices Foundation and Alfred Publishing Co

FOCUS

- Singing Development
- Concepts: pitch, rhythm

TEACHING OBJECTIVES

- To further develop the sound quality of singing
- To be able to control the starting pitch of a song
- To be able to use 'stick notation' for **ta** [crotchet/ quarter note symbol] and **teh-teh** [two quaver/ eighth notes symbol]
- To read and notate 'stick notation'

WHAT IS GOING TO HAPPEN?

- Learning how to open up the singing sound and sustain the vowels
- Individuals change the starting pitch for the consecutive performance of the same song and compare it as higher or lower
- Rhythm phrases in 'stick notation' are read and performed
- Rhythm phrases are written using 'stick notation'

SONGS

Singing Development Songs: tone 2

Heno, heno, hen blant bach [page 123]

Sorida [page 148]

Songs for rhythm and pitch activities

Double, double [page 117]

Engine, engine [page 118]

Here sits a fat cat [page 124] *

High, low, chickalow [page 126]

I like coffee, I like tea [page 131]

Rain, rain, go away [page 144] *

Starlight, star bright [page 150]

HOT SONG

Funga Alafia [page 120]

LISTENING

Sangva Duva - Traditional Tibet [track 93]

GENERAL GUIDANCE

Being able to achieve a certain singing sound in any style or genre is in part having an aural perception of the sound from listening to others, but knowing how to technically manipulate and control the Singing Voice will help to make the aim possible. The Singing Development teaching objectives in this programme are intended to give singers and teachers a small insight into vocal possibilities.

For singers an awareness of all aspects of pitch is important. Is the pitch higher or lower or the same as the previous pitch or the one to come? Am I in tune with others? How do I achieve the next high note? Melody instruments are an extension of the body and usually have techniques and mechanics that will result in producing a fixed pitch, eg note A, B, C and so on. On the other hand, the Singing Voice is an internal and organic creation, entirely dependent on the aural senses and Thinking Voice to determine the pitch to be sung.

Speaking rhythm names, eg **ta teh-teh** provides us with an important link between the sounding-rhythm and the visual notation. Notation can be liberating and give independence of access to written music. The ta is the speaking name for a **crotchet** [USA: quarter note] symbol and **teh-teh** is the speaking name for two **quavers** [USA: eighth notes]

Reading and writing conventional notation requires a systematic and progressive approach that is sensitively taught. A purely theoretical and abstract approach has limited impact, whereas learning about notation from an appropriate experiential base of making music gives children a realistic chance of negotiating this aspect with success.

SET ONE Singing Development: tone or sound quality

Refer back to Unit 10 SET ONE

Class sings 'Heno, heno, hen blant bach'

- Return to the YouTube video and listen carefully to the sounds of the Welsh language.

- Consider the first syllable sound of 'Heno' [sounds like 'hair-nor'], 'EH' minus the 'H'

- Warm-up exercises. Ask the children to:

  - Feel the tip of the tongue at the back of the lower teeth

  - Relax the jaw and to put two adjacent fingers of one hand between the teeth [thumb pointing upwards] and say a long 'EH' vowel.

  - Then, together with bright eyes, to try these two things simultaneously as they sing phrases 1 and 2 to the one vowel 'EH'

- Consider the 'OR' sound of the second syllable [minus the 'n']

- Warm-up exercises. Ask the children to:

  - Feel the tip of the tongue at the back of the lower teeth

  - Slightly purse the lips in an oval shape [going into kissing mode!]

  - Relax the jaw and open the throat as though to drink

  - Then, together with bright eyes, to try these three things simultaneously as they sing phrases 1 and 2 to the one vowel 'OR'

- Class sings the whole song attempting to focus on these vowels when they arise

Class sings 'Sorida'

Refer to Unit 10 SET ONE for the singing of the EE and AH vowels

- Sing to a slow tempo; sing with just the vowels: OR - EE - AH

- Sing to a slow tempo; sing to 'Sorida', but imagine you are still singing OR - EE - AH

Listen to 'Sangya Duva'

It is unlikely that children will have heard the singing sound of Tibetan monks before. The extraordinary depth of sound has much to do with the depth of pitch achieved by these singers.

SET TWO Pitch challenge

Select any well known song from the song repertoire

- On repeat performances, sing the song to a new starting pitch

- Ask a series of leaders to start the song preferably at a new starting pitch; the class must say if the new pitch was higher or lower

It is quite possible that one or two children will find it a problem to start the song with *"Off you go!"* at a pitch different from the previous. This can be accepted and the class say that it was the same pitch

A leader may find it easier to sing the first phrase themselves as alternative to *"Off you go!"* before the class join in

Sometimes a leader will select a pitch that is too high or low for the children to sing some of the melody; this can provide a teaching point about the upper and lower limits of the Singing Voice ie the pitch range

It is helpful to change the song from time to time

Select a known song

- Class is divided into two groups

- Each group has three selected leaders; in turn each group provides a leader to set the starting pitch which their own group matches; at the end of the singing, the first leader points either up or down as an indication for the new leader of the other group to start the song for their group at a higher or lower pitch; the challenge continues back and forth between each group and a new leader

Published by The Voices Foundation and Alfred Publishing Co
© The Voices Foundation 2014

SET THREE Introducing rhythm 'stick' notation

Refer back to Unit 9 SET THREE

To a steady 'heartbeat' pulse, speak the following four beat phrases for the class to repeat:

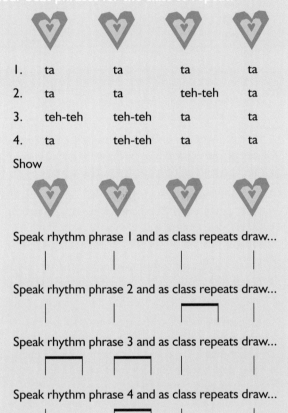

1.	ta	ta	ta	ta
2.	ta	ta	teh-teh	ta
3.	teh-teh	teh-teh	ta	ta
4.	ta	teh-teh	ta	ta

Show

Speak rhythm phrase 1 and as class repeats draw...

Speak rhythm phrase 2 and as class repeats draw...

Speak rhythm phrase 3 and as class repeats draw...

Speak rhythm phrase 4 and as class repeats draw...

SET FOUR Reading rhythm 'stick' notation'

Work with the rhythm card files on CD-2 with crotchets [quarters] and quavers [eighths] only

- With each four-beat rhythm displayed:
  - the leader marks a steady pulse quietly on a percussion instrument;
  - after four taps, the class speaks with rhythm names;
  - class immediately repeats, tapping the rhythm pattern with the speaking names 'spoken' in the Thinking Voice

Play card games

- Display a card for the class to read with Thinking Voices and to memorise; after a few moments, the card is removed, four steady taps are heard to indicate the tempo and the class speaks and taps the rhythm; the card is seen again

- Several cards are displayed; the leader taps the rhythm of one without specifying which; the class speaks the rhythm and someone identifies which was performed

SET FIVE Writing rhythm with 'stick' notation'

Each child needs to have paper, preferably lined, pencil and rubber [eraser] if possible.

A rhythm card using only crotchets [quarters] and quavers [eighths] is displayed

- Class reads and speaks the rhythm to memorise it

- Each child draws the 'stick' symbols of the card from memory

Encourage a sensible and relative proportion of the symbols; lined paper might help this; four heart drawings evenly spaced to represent the four beats could help

- Class simultaneously taps the rhythm they have drawn

- The card is shown and notations compared; if a child's notation is incorrect or the drawing can be improved on, it is suggested that they can re-draw and tap the corrected version

LEARNING OUTCOMES

- The children are increasingly aware of how the singing sound can be manipulated

- The children can adjust the starting pitch of the same song, higher or lower, in repeat performances

- The children are able to read and perform short rhythm phrases with 'stick notation', using speaking names and tapping

- The children can draw the 'stick notation' of a short rhythm phrase and perform it

Published by The Voices Foundation and Alfred Publishing Co
© The Voices Foundation 2014

FOCUS

- Performing: two-part singing
- Concepts: pitch, texture

TEACHING OBJECTIVES

- To add a third singing name, **lah**, to **soh** and **me**
- To work aurally with **lah soh me** [l-s-m] with supporting handsigns
- To improvise pitch using **lah soh me**
- To introduce the early stages leading to two-part singing

WHAT IS GOING TO HAPPEN?

- The singing name, **lah**, is introduced using several known songs
- The **lah** handsign is introduced
- Relevant song phrases are sung to singing names
- Children 'play' the 'Singing Piano'
- With guidance and examples, individuals improvise pitch to a given rhythm using **lah soh me**
- Singing as two groups where each sings a different musical part, but share in the same song [two-part texture]
- Using and listening to the so-called 'drone' in music

SONGS

Songs using the singing names, lah, soh and me

- *Apple tree* [page 108]
- **Bounce high, bounce low** [page 109]
- **John the blacksmith** [page 134]
- **Oliver Twist** [page 138]
- **Plainie clappie** [page 142]
- *Row, boat, row* [page 146]

Songs leading to part-singing: the drone

- **High, low, chickalow** [page 126]
- **Bells in the steeple** [page 109]
- **Goblins are around tonight** [page 121]

HOT SONG

Baby 1 2 3 [page 108]

LISTENING

Arabian Dance – Tchaikovsky [track 94]

YouTube: 'Behind the scenes at Wallace Bagpipes' [STV] followed by 'How bagpipes are made' [RGHardie]

GENERAL GUIDANCE

This Unit adds a third sol-fa name, **lah**, to our singing names **soh** and **me**.

The song melodies provide the most secure way of singing the correct singing name and accurate intervals between consecutive notes of pitch.

The handsigns provide important help in locating the correct pitch. When used frequently in conjunction with its singing name and its singing pitch, the handsign provides an extra reference point for the aural memory.

When the children are performing, the teacher observes, listens and assesses.

Singing 'in harmony' – or parts – is a wonderful communal experience. It is the act of contributing an indispensable role to a common purpose. Each singing-part is different, but they have a unity through common musical factors eg structure, tempo and harmony. In this Unit we sow the seeds for greater opportunities later.

The 'drone' is a simple musical device that has been with music since its birth. The drone is a fundamental part of some instruments, such as bagpipes, the sitar and the hurdy-gurdy.

Published by The Voices Foundation and Alfred Publishing Co

SET ONE Introducing the singing name, lah

Sing / teach 'Oliver Twist' [see the Song page for the game]

◼ Tell the class that there are three different pitches used in this song; touching the head for the starting pitch [soh] and shoulders for the lower sound [me], the hands follow the pitch movement; when they arrive at a new pitch even higher than the 'head pitch' soh, they should put their hands above the head. The children identify the words of the song that had the new higher pitch ['use of']

Sing 'Bounce high, bounce low'

◼ Sing phrase I only to words, then to these singing names:

soh lah soh me

◼ Demonstrate these handsigns and singing names; the class repeats

    soh   **lah**   **soh**   **me**

[mouth level] [eye level]   [throat level]

Sing 'Row, boat, row'

◼ Class sings phrases I and 2 to words, then to singing names with handsigns:

soh lah soh   soh soh lah lah soh

With the repeated notes, the handsigns make a <u>slight</u> forward and back movement to indicate with the rhythm

◼ Sing 'Apple tree'

◼ Class sings phrase I only to song words

◼ Class hums the phrase and 'imagines' the singing names, knowing that the starting note is **soh**

◼ Starting on **soh**, the class sings with singing names and supporting handsigns; if helpful, repeat; you look for a child who appears to be secure and accurate in performing this:

s - s m   s - s m   s - s   l - l   s - s m

◼ Child is invited to sing the phrase to singing names with handsigns

SET TWO More lah - soh - me song phrases

Here we have song phrases that contain

the **me - lah** interval	eg	soh **me lah** soh
and the **lah - me** interval	eg	soh **lah me** soh

Class sings 'Thumb clapping'

◼ To a slower tempo, class sings phrases I and 2 to words; repeats to humming

◼ Starting on **soh**, class sings the phrases to singing names with supporting handsigns; repeat if helpful; you look for a child who appears to be secure and accurate in performing this:

s m s m s - s m - l s m

◼ Child is invited to sing the phrase to singing names with handsigns

Class sings 'John the blacksmith'

◼ To a slower tempo, class sings phrase I to words, then immediately repeats with humming

◼ Starting on **soh**, class sings the phrases to singing names with supporting handsigns; repeat if helpful; you look for a child who appears to be secure and accurate in performing this:

s - s s - s l - m s l - m s

◼ Child is invited to sing the phrase to singing names with handsigns

Published by The Voices Foundation and Alfred Publishing Co
© The Voices Foundation 2014

SET THREE 'Playing' the Singing Piano

The Singing Piano

- Three small groups are organised in a suitable space; each is assigned a different singing-name:

- Class sings phrase 1 only of 'Bounce high, bounce low'

- Class sings phrase 1 to singing names [s l s m]

- You sign phrase 1 to the Singing Piano and the three groups sing their allotted singing name; individuals can 'play' phrase 1 by signing

New phrases to play on the Singing Piano

s m s l s   s l s m s   s l s l s   s s l l s

- Handsign each of the above examples in turn, for the class to sing; a 'player' then steps forward to sign the phrase to the Singing Piano who sing their allotted note

Improvising new phrases

- Starting with **soh**, individual 'players' sign a short phrase for the Singing Piano; encourage the children to 'hear' with their Thinking Voice the sounds that they want before signing the Singing Piano

SET FOUR Improvising pitch to a given rhythm

The display examples here and in the rest of the Units can be found as files on CD-2. You may wish to use these to project on to a screen or simply draw your own.

Display in turn each of the four-beat rhythm phrases below; using lah, soh and me, an individual adds part of the pitch content to complete the example

- First, the class 'tunes-up' by singing 'Oliver Twist' and 'Bounce high, bounce low'

- The class 'tunes' into the three singing names; you sing **soh** and show the handsign; using the singing names, the class sings as you sign the following:

- The class taps and speaks the first rhythm phrase with rhythm words

- Everyone is asked to use their **Thinking Voice** to find a solution; handsigning with their Thinking Voice is helpful

You now invite a child to sing their solution

You may think it is helpful for the class to sing the given singing names in the example, before they look for a solution

- It is possible for a child to sing a 'correct' pitch with an incorrect singing name; if you feel this has happened, ask the child to HUM the melody only; the class sings the corrected version to singing names with supporting handsigns and the child repeats this

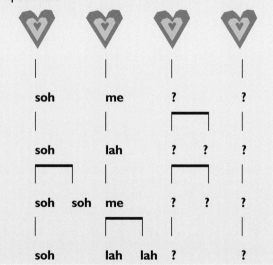

Published by The Voices Foundation and Alfred Publishing Co

SET FIVE Singing in parts: the drone

For this activity it is best that the class stands when performing so as to have better breath control

Class sings the song 'High, low, chickalow' to a lively tempo

- Class sings the word 'High', sustaining it for seven beats as the teacher counts; the note should not waver in pitch

- One group sings the sustained note [the drone] as the other group HUMS phrase 1 of the melody; the groups swap parts and repeat

- At the end of phrase 1 both parts should take a relaxed breath for phrase 2

- The complete song is performed – the melody with words and the drone with the single word 'High'

- The two groups swap parts for phrase 2

Class sings the song 'Bells in the steeple' to a lively tempo

- Class sings and sustains without wavering the first word [Bells] for eleven beats, breathes on beat 12, then repeats; the teacher counts

- Divide the class into two groups; each group tries the drone

- Starting simultaneously, one group sings the song melody while the other sings the drone; the latter sings the drone twice, breathing with the new phrase, to complete song

- The parts are swapped and the two-part performance takes place

- When confidence is achieved, ask the groups to swap parts after the first phrase

Class sings the song 'Goblins are around tonight'

- Using the first word repeatedly, sing on the starting pitch, thus:

Beat 1   2   3   4   1   2   3   4

Go - - - - - blins_____   Go - - - - - blins_____

This becomes the drone

- Use the previous procedures to develop two-part singing

SET SIX Listening: the drone

The drone is a feature of many different musical styles and traditions

In his Arabian Dance, Tchaikovsky uses the drone to suggest music of the Middle East

YouTube: The drone is a particular feature of bagpipes; bagpipes are a worldwide instrument and come in various sizes and constructions; the video visits Scotland to see how Scottish bagpipes are made

LEARNING OUTCOMES

- Children are familiar with three of the sol-fa singing names - **lah soh me** - and can work aurally with them

- Children can participate in two-part singing of melody with drone [two-part texture]

Published by The Voices Foundation and Alfred Publishing Co
© The Voices Foundation 2014

Two weeks

FOCUS

- Performing: pitch [tuned] percussion
- Concepts: pitch, rhythm

TEACHING OBJECTIVES

- To play on pitch percussion phrases from known songs
- To introduce the **ta rest** [crotchet/quarter note *rest*]
- To read and notate rhythm phrases that include the **rest** symbol, **Z**

WHAT IS GOING TO HAPPEN?

- Several melodic phrases using the singing names **lah soh me** [s-l-s-m / s-m-s-l-s] from known songs are played on pitch percussion
- Working aurally, the **rest** is found in song phrases and a recorded piece
- The **rest** symbol, **Z** is shown and read in rhythm phrases using 'stick notation'
- Phrases using the new symbol are notated

SONGS

For performing on pitch percussion

Apple tree [page 108]

John the blacksmith [page 134]

Plainie clappie [page 142]

Row, boat, row [page 146]

For identifying the **ta rest**

Bow wow wow [page 110] * [3]

Fire! Fire! [page 120] [4]

Obwisana [page 136] [2]

Pease pudding hot [page 140] [3]

Rain is falling down [page 143] * [3]

Row, boat, row [page 146] [3]

HOT SONG

LISTENING

The Typewriter - Leroy Anderson [track 95]

YouTube: 'The Typewriter' played by Martin Breinschmid

GENERAL GUIDANCE

This Unit extends the scope of melodies and skills used when playing pitch [tuned] percussion. The guidance given in SET THREE for which beater to use for each note, left or right hand held, is just one solution. The choice is partly guided by the speed of rhythmic movement, partly by economy of arm-wrist movement and partly a matter of player preference. There can, and will be variations from player to player. One of the most important considerations is that the player is working with the two beaters and not playing all the notes with just one.

Rhythm can be both sound and silence. Rhythmic silence in a musical phrase is known by the word rest and shown by the symbol **Z**. In fact, the silence is very much an active aspect of rhythm in a phrase.

Published by The Voices Foundation and Alfred Publishing Co
© The Voices Foundation 2014

SET ONE Locating the rhythmic silence in song phrases

Sing / teach a song from the list for identifying the ta rest

- Sing and tap the rhythm of the chosen song

- On arriving at a moment of 'no singing' [silence] let the hands touch the shoulders

- Using the Thinking Voice, tap the rhythmic sounds on hands and the rhythmic silences - the **rests** - on the shoulders

A rhythmic **rest** often occurs at the end of a phrase, including the end of the melody, as well as elsewhere. The number of **rests** to be found in each song is shown against the titles in SONGS list

SET TWO The rhythmic rest with no speaking name

They tap phrases1 and 2, speaking the rhythm names; at each rhythmic silence, the class touch their shoulders and 'button-their-lips'

ta ta ta [silence!] teh-teh teh-teh ta [silence!]

Ask the class to tap the rhythm and gesture the silence of phrase 1 only

Class repeats this, but as they do so, you draw for all to see:

| | | | Z |

Phrase 2 is similarly performed and you draw:

```
┌─┐   ┌─┐      |      Z
```

Ask six children to show this phrase as 'Rhythm People', thus:

Tell the class that the Z is the symbol for a crotchet [quarter] rest [silence]

- Using the above teaching procedure, take the first phrase of known songs from the SONGS list and with the class, aurally find its rhythm to notate using 'stick' notation; ask the children to draw on paper; one child could simultaneously notate on a board; the phrases could be formed by groups of 'Rhythm People'

- You can check the results against the rhythm notation used in the Song pages; at the moment the rhythms should only appear as 'stick' notation as in the previous examples

SET THREE Playing more tunes on pitch [tuned] percussion

The forearms and flexible wrists play a vital part in performing with beaters [mallets]; see the Mahalo videos for guidance about holding beaters and the most helpful height relationship of arms, wrists, beaters and instrument bars

Warm-up to wrist action: see the exercises in Unit 5 SET TWO

Published by The Voices Foundation and Alfred Publishing Co
© The Voices Foundation 2014

- Class performs phrase I only to singing names with supporting handsigns thus:

soh - soh   me   soh - soh   me

soh- soh   lah - lah   soh - soh   me

- With the class kneeling in a circle or several circles, let:

left leg = me
right leg = soh
floor to side of right leg = lah

- Starting with left hand the children tap with alternating hands while singing to the singing names thus:

Singing name: **s s m s s m s s l l s s m**
Hand: **L R L L R L L R L R L R L**

- Recall the videos

- All sing the 'Apple tree' song phrase to singing names and perform with beaters on the legs - the 'pitch percussion bars' - as above

- Children 'tune' to the pitch percussion, singing and playing:

E [me]   G [soh]   A [lah]
[Left leg] [Right leg] [Floor to side of right leg]

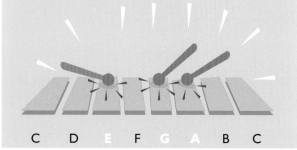

C   D   E   F   G   A   B   C

- Starting on G, children sing the song to instrument names and play their 'instrument' thus:

G G E G G E   G G A A G G E
L R L L R L   L R L R L R L

- Children play the song melody on available pitch percussion as the class listens or supports, eg quietly singing the instrument names

Suggestion for a concert performance:

- Instruments play the melody - children sing the song - both instruments and voices perform

The same teaching process can be used for phrases from other songs in the SONG list

SET FOUR Listening to 'The Typewriter'

- What is a typewriter? Would children like to research this?

- Having found out some facts about the machine, can the children understand what is happening in this lively piece?

- How many bell rings are there?

YouTube: Among several videos of this piece, there is at the moment a brilliant posting of Martin Breinschmid playing an actual typewriter

LEARNING OUTCOMES

- Children can identify the silent crotchet [quarter note] *rest* in song phrases and also read and notate phrases using it

- Children can play on pitch [tuned] percussion instruments, song melodies using three different notes

Published by The Voices Foundation and Alfred Publishing Co
© The Voices Foundation 2014

FOCUS

- Singing Development
- Concept: phrase structure

TEACHING OBJECTIVES

- To sing with sustained sounds that connect smoothly and easily
- To identify, count and label phrases in songs [structure]
- To compose rhythm pieces

WHAT IS GOING TO HAPPEN?

- Singing with a series of connected sounds known as *legato* singing
- Working with songs to illustrate 4-phrase structures, both rhythmic and melodic examples
- Using a guided approach to compose a four-phrase rhythm piece, starting with improvising, then writing the piece with notation

SONGS

Singing Development Songs: tone 3

Michael row the boat ashore [page 135]

Now the day is over [page 135]

Summer goodbye [page 151]

For identifying phrase structure

Fire! Fire! [AB] [page 120]

Goblins are around tonight [AABA] [page 121]

John the blacksmith [AA] [page 134]

Old King Glory [ABC] [page 137]

HOT SONG

Chicken on a fence post [page 115]

LISTENING

O Pastor Animarum - Saint Hildegard [track 97]

Under the Greenwood Tree - Anon [track 96]

GENERAL GUIDANCE

The Singing Voice is in essence a 'wind instrument': the sound is produced by the use of air. We can control the flow of air to produce a longer or shorter sound; we can sing from one pitch to another without interrupting the air flow - *legato* or smooth singing - or we can interrupt the air flow to produce a series of shorter sounds - *non legato*, detached sounds, or *staccato*. Some songs will require only *legato* singing and some will require a mixture of *legato* and *non legato* singing. The style and genre of the song will determine what is appropriate. The singer needs to be able to respond accordingly.

In Unit 13 we discovered that the music in two phrases of a song's melody might be the same while the music in the others would be different. A phrase might be repeated while another was not. Also, we learned that a phrase has a duration or length measured by its number of beats. Usually the phrases in a song were of the same duration or length, but sometimes one phrase would be of a different length.

It is possible to identify the composition of phrases in a melody by labelling them with alphabetical letters. The first phrase is labelled A. If the music of that phrase occurs a further time, it is also labelled A. The next different phrase after A is labelled B, the next C, and so on. The labels define the phrase structure.

Improvising music means that the performer will make many spontaneous decisions about what to play in the way of pitch, rhythm and dynamics. However, the improvising is unlikely to be entirely free and without structure. A great deal of understanding, skill, knowledge and experience will be the basis of the performance. There is probably an understood structural base, especially when improvising with other musicians. At its best, it sounds like a spontaneous composition.

Composing has its roots in improvising, but whereas spontaneous improvising lasts for one performance and then is largely forgotten, unless recorded or it lingers in the memory, composing is about formalising musical ideas by notating them on paper. This means that the piece can be performed many times with very similar results.

SET ONE Singing Development: legato singing

Listen to 'O Pastor Animarum'

■ Ask the class to notice how each sound from the singer melts into the next; the sounds flow like pearls on a necklace, individual notes, but linked together by a continuous string of sound

The seamless sound is called *legato* [smooth] singing and is the result of a consistent and supportive breath; focus on the vowels and careful listening.

The class sings 'Michael row the boat ashore'

■ They sing phrase 1 only to 'AH'; as they do so, they 'draw' with both arms a large circle in the air before them, starting from the top, arms moving slowly in opposite directions, meeting at the bottom for the end of the phrase; the singing has to match the smoothness and continuous motion of the arms

The actions are done to encourage the singers to sing legato

■ As before, but the class sings to 'OO'

The class sings 'Summer goodbye'

■ They sing phrases 1 and 2 of the melody with alternating vowels, 'AH - OO - AH - OO', keeping the sound unbroken through each phrase

The class sings 'Now the day is over'

■ It is sung as two phrases to the words with the class keeping a firm consistent breath support, an open throat and relaxed tongue and jaw; children sing *legato* as though they were sticking each sound onto the next with super-glue!

SET TWO Identifying the phrase structure in a melody

In Unit 13 the phrases of a song were compared as being the same or different; here we identify the phrase structure by labelling; see GENERAL GUIDANCE

Sing 'Sweetly John the bell'

This song has a melody of two phrases, each with identical rhythm and pitch

■ Class divided into two groups, sing one phrase each

■ Ask the children to compare the music of the two phrases

■ Since they are the same, each phrase is labelled A, ie A A

This song has two phrases, each being rhythmically different

■ Divided into two groups, each is asked to tap the rhythm of their allocated phrase as they perform the song using Thinking Voices

■ Ask the children whether the rhythms were the same or different

■ Since they are different, phrase 1 is labelled, A and phrase 2, B

This song has three phrases, each is different

■ Class, divided into three groups, sings one phrase each to 'nah'

■ Ask the children to compare the phrases as being same or different

■ Since they are different to each other, label the phrases, A B C

Sing 'Spinning top'

This song has four phrases where phrases 1 and 2 are repeated as phrases 3 and 4

■ Singing alternately, two groups perform the four phrases; first group sings to 'nor', second group to 'nee'

■ Ask the children to compare the music of the phrases and decide on how to label the four phrases

■ You should reach a consensus of: A B A B

Published by The Voices Foundation and Alfred Publishing Co

SET THREE Listen to recorded music and decide on the structure

Listen to 'Under the Greenwood Tree'

- What is the phrase structure? Listen several times

- Is it useful for children to identify the phrases by drawing 'rainbow' arcs with the help of pencil and paper and one person using a white board?

- Can they label their phrases? Compare their thoughts?

- Is the structure A A B C and then repeated?

SET FOUR Improvised rhythms leading to a composed piece

A guided approach to composing a rhythm piece should offer the children a 'scaffold' in which they can more easily secure success.

Always work aurally with known rhythms since the outcome is to notate the rhythms; known rhythms include the **teh-teh, ta** and the **ta** *rest* [Z].

It is helpful for everyone to feel a steady pulse before performing. The teacher using a four-tap introduction can establish this.

As a warm-up to composing, you speak four-beat rhythms for class to imitate

- Eg **ta teh-teh ta ta / teh-teh teh-teh ta [z rest]**

- Tap four-beat rhythms for class to imitate

- Eg

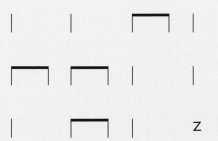

- Tap several four-beat phrases using known rhythms for the class to <u>speak</u> using rhythm names [rhythm card examples using 'stick notation' could help]

Two leaders and two groups

- Leader 1 taps a 4-beat phrase [A] for group 1 to tap and speak to rhythm names; they repeat the phrase and memorise

- Leader 2 taps a different 4-beat rhythm phrase [B] for group 2 to tap and speak to rhythm names; they repeat the phrase and memorise

- The two groups now perform the four phrase structure:

A B A B , then **A B B A**

- Individually children of both groups notate with 'stick notation' their respective rhythms

- Members of the groups exchange their notated phrase with a person in the other group

- Someone suggests a four-phrase structure - A always leads - and the piece is read from the notation and performed with tapping

- The piece is re-performed using a different tempo set by the teacher playing an introduction of four beats and to agreed dynamics

- The piece is repeated with two children each playing on an untuned percussion instrument as the class listens; child A sets the tempo, but both may select their own dynamics

- Working in pairs and using the above procedure and experience, children compose a new four phrase rhythm piece; later they perform their notated piece on untuned percussion.

LEARNING OUTCOMES

- Children are aware of *legato* singing and are striving to achieve the ability to use it

- Children can identify the phrases in a melody, count them and label them

- Children can improvise and compose four 4-beat phrases to a chosen structure

Published by The Voices Foundation and Alfred Publishing Co
© The Voices Foundation 2014

Three weeks

FOCUS

- Performing: two-part music
- Notation

TEACHING OBJECTIVES

- To read and perform rhythm notation using noteheads
- To perform music with two parts [texture]
- To combine rhythm and pitch symbols to produce melodic notation known as rhythm sol-fa

WHAT IS GOING TO HAPPEN?

- Rhythm pieces are read from notation using noteheads, memorised and performed on percussion instruments
- Working as two groups where one group taps a rhythm ostinato as the other sings the song
- Listening to music that uses ostinato as part of its structure
- Working aurally with song phrases and improvised phrases to identify their rhythm and pitch, before notating rhythm sol-fa

SONGS

Songs leading to part-singing: ostinato

Heno, heno, hen blant bach [page 123]

Spinning top [page 149]

We can sing high [page 153]

Rhythm phrases seen with noteheads

Coca-Cola went to town [page 115]

I, I, me oh my [page 131]

Pease pudding hot [page 140]

Songs with relevant rhythm sol-fa notation:

Apple tree [page 108]

Bounce high, bounce low [page 109]

Fire! Fire! [page 120]

Plainie clappie [page 142]

Row, boat, row [page 146]

HOT SONG

Jambo jam [page 133]

LISTENING

YouTube: Children's games/clapping games etc.

Pavane – Peter Warlock [track 98]

GENERAL GUIDANCE

In this book so far, the children have been using 'stick notation' for rhythm symbols. It has been possible to distinguish the crotchet [quarter note] and quaver [eighth note] symbols by the 'stick' stems only. The introduction of the minim [half note] rhythm symbol in Unit 20 necessitates the introduction of the notehead in order to distinguish the crotchet [quarter note] from the minim [half note]. Also, the note head is always used when notating pitch and rhythm together, eg melody in rhythm sol-fa.

Ostinato is another simple music device for enabling the children to take part in two-part music [two-part texture]. The fact that ostinato and drone are so markedly different from the other part, the melody, enables children to aurally distinguish the parts, not to become aurally confused, but to be clearly aware of the companion part. This aural separation is not possible when singing rounds. Rounds are best avoided until the children have more experience. Rounds performed too early in children's development can give rise to singing 'out of tune' and a tendency to poor sound quality.

The Listening example shows the children that their learning is part of the world of music, not just the classroom.

Rhythm sol-fa notation is a combination of rhythm symbols and sol-fa names shortened to the initial letter. It is a notation that is useful for the Singing Voice, but not instruments.

There are known song phrases that can be notated using rhythm sol-fa. The **First Steps** need to be carefully managed, ensuring that unhurried and adequate time is allowed. The first experiences should be satisfying and rewarding for you and the children.

Published by The Voices Foundation and Alfred Publishing Co
© The Voices Foundation 2014

SET ONE Noteheads

The display examples here and in the rest of the Units can be found as files on CD-2. You may wish to use these to project on to a screen or simply draw your own.

Noteheads are 'blobs' added to the foot of the vertical 'sticks' in rhythm notation

Show the following and ask children to copy onto paper

Encourage the class to draw:

- The notehead first, leading straight into the 'stick'
- Neatly with noteheads of a regular shape and size, quite small
- Neatly with stick lengths of a regular height

Rhythms to read and perform

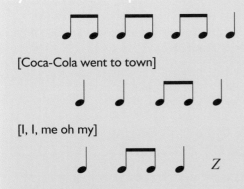

[Coca-Cola went to town]

[I, I, me oh my]

[Pease pudding hot]

- Show to the class as noteheaded rhythm notation
- Speak to rhythm names, memorise
- Perform on percussion instruments

Child improvises a 4-beat rhythm, tapping or speaking rhythm names

- Class imitates and uses rhythm names
- The rhythm is notated by each person; accuracy and legibility is compared

More examples are improvised, notated and performed on untuned percussion instruments

SET TWO Music with two parts: song melody and rhythm ostinato

Sing the song 'We can sing high'

- The class taps:

- Two groups, one to sing the song, the other to tap the above repeatedly during the singing
- Establish the tempo and singing pitch; both groups start and perform
- One group sings as several players on untuned percussion play the **rhythm ostinato**; the second group listens to both parts
- Two individuals: one sings, the other performs the **rhythm ostinato**
- The class sings the song while simultaneously tapping the **rhythm ostinato**; several children play the ostinato on percussion and do not sing
- Can a child sing and perform the ostinato simultaneously?

Sing the songs 'Spinning top' and 'Heno, heno, hen blant bach'

- To each song, perform this ostinato using the above teaching ideas

SET THREE Listening to 'Pavane'

This piece is in the style of a popular 16th century courtly dance.

The ostinato is played on a melodic instrument and the pitch is changed frequently, however the rhythm is constant throughout:

- Ask the class to practise this ostinato rhythm first with two fingers lightly tapping on the palm of the other hand, and then to add the ostinato to the Pavane as it is played.

Published by The Voices Foundation and Alfred Publishing Co
© The Voices Foundation 2014

SET FOUR Introducing rhythm sol-fa notation

When sol-fa letters appear under a notated rhythm with noteheads, it is known as rhythm sol-fa notation

Class sings the song 'Apple tree'

Class sings the words 'Apple tree, apple tree' [phrase 1]

Ask the class to read the above and sing to sol-fa

Display the following [2]:

Class sings the words 'Will your apples fall on me?' [phrase 2]

Ask the class to read the above and sing to sol-fa

Display the following [3]: phrases 1 and 2 of 'Row boat, row' and use the above procedure

Notice how the crotchet [quarter] rest sign has been replaced by the accepted publishing symbol. When writing their own music, children may continue to use the symbol Z

Display the following [4]: phrase 1 of 'Plainie clappie' and use the above procedure

SET FIVE Notating rhythm sol-fa

Children will require paper and pencil

Display example 1 in SET FOUR

- Children draw carefully what they see

  Encourage the class to draw:

  - The notehead first, leading straight into the 'stick'

  - Neatly with noteheads of a regular shape and size, quite small

  - Neatly with stick lengths of a regular height

Sing to the class example 2 in SET FOUR [NO display] to singing names

- Class sings back several times to memorise

- All speak with rhythm names and tap the rhythm

- Each draws the rhythm of the example

- Class sings the example again

- Each writes in the sol-fa letters

- Display example 2 for class to compare

Class sings the song 'Bounce high, bounce low'

- Class sings phrase 1 to words

- Each taps the rhythm and uses the Thinking Voice to decide on the rhythm and notate it

- Check

- Class hums the phrase

- Using their Thinking Voice, each child sings the phrase to sol-fa singing names with supporting handsigns

- Each person writes in the sol-fa letters under the respective noteheads

- Find a child who has drawn the notation shown below and ask that person to notate on a board for all to see and compare

SET SIX Children's singing games on YouTube

There are a number of YouTube videos, often led by children, that show a range of singing and chanting games with actions. The class may be interested to compare their own games and show others. Such videos show children that they are part of a world-wide cultural phenomenon

LEARNING OUTCOMES

- Children can notate rhythms with noteheads

- Children can perform in two-part music: melody with ostinato rhythm [two-part texture]

- Children understand the term *ostinato*

- Children can read and write rhythm sol-fa notation

Published by The Voices Foundation and Alfred Publishing Co
© The Voices Foundation 2014

Three weeks

FOCUS

- Notation
- Concept: pitch

TEACHING OBJECTIVES

- To introduce **doh** and to work aurally with **s-m-d**
- To use the tone-set **s-m-d** when improvising, memorising and reading [rhythm sol-fa]
- To understand bar lines and time signatures

WHAT IS GOING TO HAPPEN?

- Introducing the note **doh** and its supporting handsign through known song melodies
- Using **doh** with **soh** and **me** in phrases and fragments from song melodies
- Improvising melodic phrases with s-m-d
- Reading and writing in rhythm sol-fa using s-m-d
- Songs with metres of 2 or 4 are sung with appropriate actions, helping children feel the strong and weak pulses
- Children are shown how bar lines are used in notation to place the music into bars

SONGS

Songs using soh - me - doh [s-m-d]

Bells in the steeple [page 109]

Chest, chest, knee, toe [phrases 1 and 2] [page 114]

Jambo jam [page 133]

Sorida [page 148]

Songs for time signatures and bar lines

Acha bacha [page 107] 4

Coca-Cola went to town [page 115] 2

Double, double [page 117] 2

Spinning top [page 149] 4

HOT SONG

Select a request

LISTENING

Tempo's Boogie - Hampton [track 99]

GENERAL GUIDANCE

The sol-fa singing name, doh, introduces a pitch that, in this Unit at least, is lower than soh and me. When introducing a new singing name always work first with the given song examples to secure the intervals accurately.

The notation we use today took centuries to evolve. It was partly driven on by the increasing complexity of music, the development of printing and the desire for a common system that musicians could work with across the western world. One of these developments was the emergence of time signatures and bar lines.

SET ONE Introducing doh and handsign

Sing the song 'Chest, chest, knee, toe'

- Class sings phrases 1 and 2 to singing names starting on **soh** with supporting handsigns, thus:

Chest	chest	knee	toe	[repeat]
soh	**soh**	**me**	**?**	[repeat]

- What do the children experience on the last word? The last note presents with a pitch lower than **me**; this is to be sung as **doh**

- Sing the phrases again with the new name and its handsign:

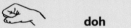 **doh** [chest height]

- Here are the three handsigns for these phrases:

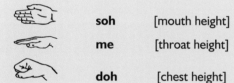

soh [mouth height]

me [throat height]

doh [chest height]

SET TWO Song phrases using soh me doh

The following song melodies use the singing names **soh me doh** only. Each melody starts on **soh**; **doh** is the lowest pitch of the three

Everyone should use the relevant handsign when singing to sol-fa names

Sing 'Sorida'

- Class sings phrase 1 to sol-fa with a <u>slower tempo</u> starting on **soh**

- Which of the three syllables of the word Sorida always has doh? [- da]

[s m d s m d m d m d]

Sing 'Jambo jam'

- Class sings phrase 1 to sol-fa with a <u>slower tempo</u> starting on **soh**

[s m s m d m d m d m d]

Sing 'Bells in the steeple'

- Class sings phrase 1 of the melody with supporting handsigns, <u>starting on **doh** and to a slow tempo</u>

[d d d m m m s s s m]

- Ask the class to sing phrase 2, starting on **doh**, without visual display; spot an individual who sang and signed correctly and ask the child to demonstrate

[d m s d m s d m s d]

- Sing both phrases consecutively to singing names with supporting handsigns; keep the tempo quite slow

Playing the melody of 'Bells in the steeple' on pitch [tuned] percussion

Let doh = F; me = A; soh = C

C	D	E	G	A	B	
		doh		**me**		**soh**

- Class sing phrase 1 only to singing names starting on instrument pitch F:

[d d d m m m s s s m]

- Class are told that: doh = F; me = A; soh = C

- They sing phrase 1 several times to instrument letter names:

F F F A A A C C C A

Published by The Voices Foundation and Alfred Publishing Co
© The Voices Foundation 2014

Each child holds the left hand like this:

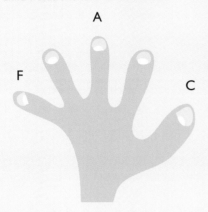

They are told the small finger is their F bar; the tallest/middle finger is the A bar and the thumb is the C bar

The index finger of the right hand points to the 'finger bars' as the letter names are sung

One player is assigned to each pitch percussion instrument

Repeat phrase 1 with the players 'finger pointing the bars'

Using two beaters alternately, the instruments are played as the song is sung first to letter names and then to song words

Develop phrase 2 in the same way

Play and sing both phrases

SET THREE Improvising pitch sequences

To 'tune up', sing the song 'Jambo'

Starting on **soh**, you improvise a short pitch sequence, signing as you do so; the children sing singing names from your signs

The sequences should be short and move slowly - see examples below

Do the above, starting on **doh**

Let children be leaders

Examples of pitch sequences:

s m s d / d m s s / d m d s

SET FOUR Rhythm sol-fa

Class will need paper and pencil

Using the following, you perform an example

Examples:

1. s   s   m   s   d

2. d   d   m   s

3. d   m   s   s   d

Class imitates each example several times, with a tapped pulse / with a tapped rhythm / with handsigns; when memorised, the rhythm is notated, then singing names are added

To a displayed 4-beat rhythm, a child improvises the pitch, starting on **soh** or **doh**

'Tune up' with the help of a s-m-d song; reading from a leader's handsigns, the class sings to singing names

Display a simple 4-beat rhythm, eg

Everyone reads and taps the rhythm phrase twice

The child to improvise 'tunes up' by singing and signing s-m-d

The child chooses to start on either **soh** or **doh**

Encourage the improviser to give brief thinking time and to hear in silence [Thinking Voice] how they might proceed

Child sings to singing names with supporting handsigns; if 'correct', the child repeats, and afterwards, the class repeats

IMPORTANT! The pitch of the improvised phrase can be perfectly valid, but the child may use an incorrect singing name for a note. In this case, work with the pitch that is sung and correct the singing name. Humming the note or notes in question or, indeed, the whole phrase, can help to find the correct name[s]

Published by The Voices Foundation and Alfred Publishing Co
© The Voices Foundation 2014

Working individually, or in pairs for confidence, class notates the new phrase in rhythm sol-fa; help is offered where necessary

The class collectively sings what they have written; they can compare

SET FIVE Strong and weak beats

This is a direct follow-on to Unit 7 SET FIVE

'Spinning top' has a metre of 4 beats: **strong** – weak – weak – weak

Class sings 'Spinning top'

Follow the teaching sequence below with the help of the visual supports

1.

    Spin - ning   top goes   round and   round

    List - en   to   its   hum - ming sound

Display the four hearts representing the pulse

Class marks the pulse and sings phrases 1 and 2

2.

    Spin - ning   top goes   round and   round

    List - en   to   its   hum - ming sound

Now display the four hearts as above

For the large pulse the class slaps the upper legs as they sit on chairs; for the smaller hearts they tap two 'potato' fists

They sing phrases 1 and 2 as they tap

3.

Display the above for the class to read

With the actions for pulse used in 2., the class reads and speaks to rhythm names

4.

Display the above

The class performs with pulse actions used in 2. and 3.

Class taps the rhythm

Explain that:

$\frac{4}{4}$ is termed a **time signature** and says that the music has a metre of four beats to each bar

| is a bar line and that the music between two bar lines is called a **bar** [USA: measure]

The chant '*Acha bacha*' would also be notated with a $\frac{4}{4}$ time signature

5.

Display; class reads and performs

Individuals perform 4. and 5. on untuned percussion

Published by The Voices Foundation and Alfred Publishing Co

SET SIX Songs/chants with a metre of 2

'Double double' has a metre of 2: **strong** – weak – **strong** – weak

Follow the teaching sequence in SET FIVE

1. Phrase 1 and 2

| Dou - ble | dou - ble | this | this |
| Dou - ble | dou - ble | that | that |

2.

[leg slap]	[fist tap]	[leg slap]	[fist tap]
Dou - ble	dou - ble	this	this
Dou - ble	dou - ble	that	that

3.

4. Therefore the time signature is $\frac{2}{4}$

The song 'Coca-Cola' would also be notated with a $\frac{2}{4}$ time signature

SET SEVEN Listening to Lionel Hampton

Listen to Lionel Hampton's 'Tempo's Boogie'

- Ask the class what they think the metre of this piece is [4]

- As they listen, the class feels the metre of 4 with these actions:

  1   2   3   4   **1**   2   3   4

  clap   tap   tap   tap   clap   tap   tap   tap

As above, but actions with a partner [hand clap own hands x 1, slap partner's hands x 3]

LEARNING OUTCOMES

- Children work aurally with **soh me doh**

- Children can read and perform rhythm sol-fa examples using **soh**, **me** and **doh**.

- Children are aware of metre, time signatures, bar lines and bars [measures]

- Children can read and perform rhythm notation with time signatures and bar lines.

Published by The Voices Foundation and Alfred Publishing Co
© The Voices Foundation 2014

Three - four weeks

FOCUS

- Performing: two-part singing
- Concepts: pitch, rhythm

TEACHING OBJECTIVES

- To introduce the minim [half note] rhythm value
- To perform two-part music: song melody with melodic *ostinato*
- To introduce and use the note **ray**
- To use the tone-set **m-r-d**, to sing song phrases, read rhythm sol-fa, to use memory and recall and to improvise

WHAT IS GOING TO HAPPEN?

- Identifying song rhythms that include the minim [half note]
- Speaking rhythm phrases that use the minim [half note] speaking-name: **ta - - a**
- Adding a melodic *ostinato* to a song melody to give a two-part piece
- Songs using the tone-set m-r-d are sung and the melodic shapes are shown simultaneously with hand movements
- The note 'ray' and its supporting handsign are introduced
- Relevant song phrases are sung to sol-fa [me-ray-doh]
- Phrases written with rhythm sol-fa notation are read and performed

SONGS

To introduce the minim [half note]

Heno, heno, hen blant bach [page 123]

I've been to Harlem [page 132]

Salani [page 146]

We can sing high [page 153]

To introduce ray

Have you ever, ever? [page 122]

I have lost the cupboard key [page 130]

One for the mouse [page 138]

Rain is falling down [page 143]

Suo gân [page 152]

HOT SONG

LISTENING

Ostinato – Gustav Holst [track 100]

GENERAL GUIDANCE

The minim [half note] has twice the <u>durational length</u> of the crotchet [quarter note] and four times that of the quaver [eighth note].

Melodic *ostinato* is another simple music device for enabling the children to take part in two-part music. The fact that one of the two parts is an *ostinato* [a repetitive short motif; in jazz, a riff] makes that part markedly different from the other, the song melody. This enables children to easily distinguish the parts, not to become aurally confused, but to be clearly aware of the companion part. This aural separation is not possible when singing rounds. As has been previously pointed out, singing rounds is best avoided until the children have more experience.

Another sol-fa singing name, **ray**, is introduced.

Notation is not an end in itself: it enables further 'live' music-making to take place, such as reading and performing new song phrases, and is a tool for composing new melodic phrases.

Published by The Voices Foundation and Alfred Publishing Co

SET ONE The minim [half note] in song phrases

Sing the song 'We can sing high'

- Each heart represents a pulse

- Class taps the pulse while singing in one breath phrase 1 -

We	can	sing	high_____
We	can	sing	low_____

- Sustain 'high' and 'low' for two full beats each

- How many taps were made for each word ? [2]

- Class sings and <u>taps the rhythm</u> on the palm of a hand

IMPORTANT! For 'high' and 'low', the tapping-hand taps, the palm-hand closes over the fingers and both 'bounce' to the child's right for beat 2 to represent the duration of the two-beat note

- Class speaks the rhythm names as they tap the pulse, thus:

teh - teh	ta	ta - - a_____
teh - teh	ta	ta - - a_____

ta - a is the speaking name used for a sound of two beats duration in Simple Time – the **minim** [half note]

- Display this for children to read and tap:

IMPORTANT! Remember the 'tap-and-hold and bounce' on the tapped palm for ta - a for the minim

- Show:

Class reads, taps and says the rhythm names

Class sings the song 'I've been to Harlem'

- Class sings and taps the phrase 'Sailing East, sailing West'

- Taps and says:

ta   ta   ta - - a   ta   ta   ta - - a

- Show:

- Class reads and says the rhythm names

- Class sings and taps the phrase 'Sailing over the ocean'

- Taps and says:

ta   ta   ta   teh-teh   ta - - a   ta - - a

- Show:

- Class reads and says the rhythm names

- Both phrases are now performed consecutively

- Percussion instruments perform: the minim [half note] is of two-beat duration and needs a sustaining sound; metal instruments will ring on; a tambourine tapped and shaken; most melodic instruments can sustain the minim [half note] duration, but will have to play a pitch

Class sings the song 'Salani'

- Sings and taps phrases 1 and 2

- Display:

- Class reads, taps and speaks the rhythm names

- Individuals play from memory on untuned percussion selecting their own tempo and dynamics

The notation symbol for the minim [half note] rest is as follows:

- In simple time notation, for example:

SET TWO Notating song phrases

Children require paper and pencil

Sing the song 'Hello, hello, heh blah haa'

- Class sings and taps phrases 1 and 2 [see the phrase marks in the SONGS notation]

- Class taps and speaks the rhythm names, thus:

ta   ta   ta   ta   ta   ta   ta - - a
[repeat for phrase 2]

- Display four empty bars with a time signature and ask the class to copy

- Class speak phrase 1 to rhythm names and notate; compare and check for accuracy and then ask them to notate phrase 2

- The phrases are notated thus:

Encourage legible notation where note-heads are of comparable size and the 'stick' lengths are comparable in length

- Children exchange their notated phrases with others and together the class performs to tapping and playing on untuned percussion

SET THREE Two-part singing: melodic ostinato

Sing the song 'I've been to Harlem'

- You sing this melodic phrase several times [*ostinato*] with supporting handsigns; class copies:

d   d   d   s   s   s   m

- Organise two groups, one to sing the song, the other to sing and sign the **melodic ostinato**

- Establish the tempo and starting pitch; both groups start and perform

- The groups swap parts and perform again

SET FOUR Listening to Holst's 'Ostinato'

The melodic *ostinato* in this piece has a small number of notes moving rapidly in a circular-like pattern quite high up in pitch.

- Ask the class to listen for the *ostinato* that starts the piece and to see if they can 'hold on' to it throughout despite other melodies being added.

SET FIVE Introducing the singing name, ray

Class sings 'One for the mouse'

- You sing: **me ray ray doh** [phrase 1]

- Class imitates

- You sing phrase 1 to singing names with handsigns, thus:

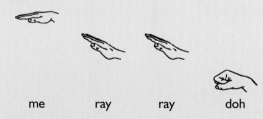

me   ray   ray   doh

- Class imitates

- You sing phrases 1 and 2 to singing names and supporting handsigns

- Class imitates

- Class sings phrase 3 to words ['One will rot' etc]

- You sing with supporting handsigns the following:

m   r   d   r   r   m   m   r   r   d

- Class imitates several times

Published by The Voices Foundation and Alfred Publishing Co
© The Voices Foundation 2014

SET SIX Other Song phrases

You sing with supporting handsigns:

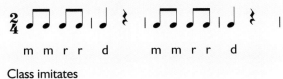

m m r r d   m m r r d

Class imitates

You sing with supporting handsigns:

d r m   r d r   d r m   r m d

Class imitates

You sing with supporting handsigns:

d d m m d d m   d d m m r m

Class imitates

SET SEVEN Reading rhythm sol-fa

Class sings 'Have you ever, ever, ever?'

- Display the following for the children to read these examples:

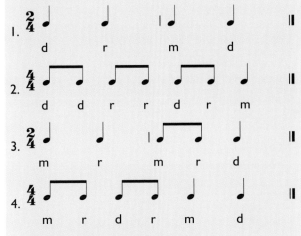

- Working with each example in turn:

  - The rhythm is read and tapped / spoken with rhythm names

  - The pitch is established by you singing with supporting handsigns:

    doh ray me for examples 1 and 2

    me ray doh for examples 3 and 4

- Class imitates

- You sing the first note of the example using *'Off you go!'*

- Class reads and sings

- Groups, pairs and individuals have the opportunity to sing one or more of the examples

LEARNING OUTCOMES

- Children can aurally identify, read and notate the minim [half] rhythm

- Children sing in two-part music, song melody and melodic *ostinato*

- Children can read and sing rhythm sol-fa notation containing the new singing name, **ray**

Published by The Voices Foundation and Alfred Publishing Co
© The Voices Foundation 2014

Three weeks

FOCUS

- Performing: two-part singing, two-part pitch percussion playing
- Concept: pitch

TEACHING OBJECTIVES

- To sing music with two voice-parts
- To work vocally and with pitch instruments on tone-sets formed from l-s-m-r-d
- To play song phrases on pitch percussion
- To play music with two instrumental parts [texture]
- To be able to perform, listen out for and understand the music device known as *drone*

WHAT IS GOING TO HAPPEN?

- Working as two groups singing music with two-voice parts: melody with ostinato drone and overlapping phrases
- Singing song phrases to sol-fa that use the tone-sets drawn from l-s-m-r-d
- Playing song melody on pitch percussion
- Playing song melody with drone
- Listening to recorded music that features the drone

SONGS

For two-part singing

Allundé alluya [page 107]

Engine, engine [page 118]

Hill an' gully ride-a [page 127]

Hot cross buns [page 127]

For two-part instrument playing

Row, boat, row [page 146]

One for the mouse [page 138]

For various tone-sets drawn from l-s-m-r-d

Apple tree [l-s-m] [page 108]

I like coffee, I like tea [s-m] [page 131]

One for the mouse [page 138]

Rain is falling down [m-r-d] [page 143] *

Salut! Ça va? [s-m-r-d] [page 147]

HOT SONG

LISTENING

Chinese Dance – Tchaikovsky [track 101]

Musette – J.S. Bach [track 102]

GENERAL GUIDANCE

A tone-set is a group of sol-fa singing names used within a song melody, eg 'Have you ever, ever, ever?' has a tone-set of m-r-d; 'Apple tree' has a tone-set of l-s-m

In a piece where there are two simultaneous performing parts required and the musical content is individually different, then the music is said to be two-part music. Two-part vocal music may take various forms, but a melody accompanied by a single-note drone is an example. A melody with a rhythm ostinato is another. Similarly, two instruments each playing a musical part with different content are performing a piece in two-parts.

Drone is a simple musical device for accompanying a melodic part or parts [see Unit 15]. Drone - a continuous single pitch, often with a repetitive rhythm [*ostinato*] - has been part of music for thousands of years. It can be heard in Buddhist chant, folk dance music and orchestral music.

Published by The Voices Foundation and Alfred Publishing Co
© The Voices Foundation 2014

SET ONE Two-part vocal music

Class sings 'Engine, engine'

- Class is divided into two groups

- The four phrases of the song are divided between the two groups so that they sing alternately

- Group A sings phrase 1, but instead of stopping when phrase 2 is sung by the other group, group A sustains the last note during phrase 2; at the end of phrase two, group A resumes phrase 3 of the melody and group B sustains its end note; for phrase 4, group A sustains its final note as group B sings phrase 4

Singing a song phrase followed by a sustained note requires the children to focus on good breath control and to support the held-note carefully; quieter singing will help these challenges enormously!

Class sings 'Allundé alluya'

- This Swahili prayer is first sung by two class groups as a 'call-and-response' song

- The 'call' and 'response' groups each in turn sustain the last note of their phrases as the other group sings the following phrase

Class sings 'Hill an' gully ride-a'

- Class is divided into two groups

- Group A sings the complete song

- Group B sings repetitively the 'response' phrase: 'hill an' gully'

- It is suggested that both groups first sing the song, then immediately group B sings the response phrase repetitively as a rhythmic drone as group A repeats the song part

Class sings the new song 'Hot cross buns'

- The class is aurally taught this melodic ostinato:

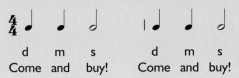

d	m	s	d	m	s
Come	and	buy!	Come	and	buy!

- The class perform as two groups

- It is suggested that both groups first sing the song, then immediately one group repeats the song melody and the other simultaneously sings the melodic ostinato, 'Come and buy'

SET TWO Tone-sets

Sing 'I like coffee, I like tea'

The melodic part is built out of two pitches only, **soh** and **me**, so has a tone-set of s - m

- The class sings phrase 1 to words, then to singing names with supporting handsigns; [**s s m m s s m**] phrase 2 has the same melody

- Tell the class that the song has a tone-set of **soh** and **me**

Sing 'Apple tree'

This song uses three pitches only, **lah**, **soh** and **me**, so has a tone-set of l - s - m

- The class sings phrase 1 to words, then to singing names with supporting handsigns; [**s s m s s m s s l l s s m**]

- Tell the class that the song has a tone-set of **lah**, **soh** and **me**

Sing the song 'Rain is falling down'

This song uses three pitches only, **me**, **ray** and **doh**, so has a tone-set of m - r - d

- The class sings phrases 1 and 2 to words, then to singing names; [**m m r r d   m m r r d**]

- Based on phrases 1 and 2 ask the class to say what the tone-set of the song is [m - r - d]

- Sing the whole song to words, then repeat to sol-fa singing names

Published by The Voices Foundation and Alfred Publishing Co
© The Voices Foundation 2014

This question-and-answer greeting uses four pitches, **soh**, **me**, **ray** and **doh**, so has tone-set of s - m - r - d

Divide the class into two groups

To words, group A sings phrase 1, group B phrase 2

The groups are told they must find the singing names for their own phrase

The groups perform the song to humming

The groups 'perform' the singing names using their Thinking Voices and supporting handsigns

The groups consult among themselves as to what they will use by way of singing names

The groups or their selected leaders, sing to singing names with handsigns;

The question phrase = **s m s m**

The answer phrase = **m r r r d**

"Then what is the tone-set of this song?" [s - m - r - d]

SET THREE Two-part instrumental music

Several pitch percussion instruments are needed, each equipped with a suitable pair of beaters. The instruments should ideally have an alto-tenor range to match the children's singing pitch.

Always encourage the players to use both beaters and, when sensible, to use them alternately.

Starting on the instruments' G pitch, the class sings 'Row, boat, row'

■ Tell the class the song has the tone-set: l - s - m and starts with **soh**

■ They now sing the song several times to sol-fa singing names with supporting handsigns

■ Class and selected instrument players are told that:

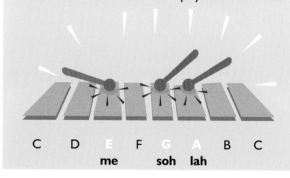

C	D	E	F	G	A	B	C
		me		**soh**	**lah**		

■ Rest of class hold left hand like this:

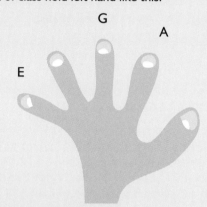

■ The index finger of the right hand points to the 'finger-bars' and the players point the bars on the instrument as the letter names are sung:

G A G / G G A A G / G A G E G A G

■ Repeat with the players using beaters on the bars as the class sing the letter names

■ Once the melody is confidently played, ask one instrument to play it without vocal support and another to play repeated Cs - a drone - in time to the pulse

Class sings 'One for the mouse'

■ Display:

m r r d   m r r d

m r d r r m m r r d

■ Class reads and sings

■ The rhythm sol-fa is sung with the instrument A being the starting note

■ They now sing to pitch percussion letters where:

■ me = A

■ ray = G

■ doh = F

Published by The Voices Foundation and Alfred Publishing Co
© The Voices Foundation 2014

With 'finger bars' of the left hand like this:

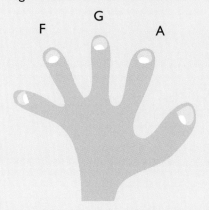

The index finger of the right hand points to the 'finger-bars' and the players point the bars on the instrument as the letter names are sung:

A G G F / A G G F / A G F G G A A G G F

Repeat with the players using beaters on the bars as the class sing the letter names

Once the melody is confidently played, ask one instrument to play it without vocal support and another to play repeated Fs to this rhythm ostinato:

This can be taught aurally; initially the class could assist the player by tapping this as a rhythm ostinato

SET FOUR Listening to music with drone

Tchaikovsky's 'Chinese Dance' from his music for the ballet 'The Nutcracker'[1892] features two bassoons - a wind instrument with a lower pitch range - playing jumpy-like drones to a dancing piccolo and flute

Ask the children to listen to the bassoons throughout

Next to listen to the high pitch and the lively antics of the flute and its even higher pitch version, the piccolo

Ask them to focus their listening on both the bassoons and the flute and piccolo

What other types of instrument are detectable? ['warbling' clarinets; plucked stringed instruments]

J.S. Bach wrote the Musette as one of a collection of pieces for his wife, Anna Magdalena, in the 1720s. A musette was a French bagpipe popular in court circles at the time. Like other bagpipes, it could sound a drone as a melody was played.

Ask the children to listen to the bouncy lower notes - the drone - as a lively part skips along above

The drone stops at some points: can the children raise their hands when this happens and lower when the drone resumes?

From its initial pitch the drone moves to another pitch and back again: can the children raise a hand when this happens?

LEARNING OUTCOMES

Children can sing vocally in two-parts using overlapping phrases and melodic ostinato

Children know that the pitch of the different notes used in a melody can be collated and identified in sol-fa names as a tone-set

Children can play a simple song melody and a drone on two pitch percussion instruments

Children can listen to recorded music using the drone and focus on this and other features

Published by The Voices Foundation and Alfred Publishing Co
© The Voices Foundation 2014

Three weeks

FOCUS

- Performing: singing
- Notation

TEACHING OBJECTIVES

- To read, sing and learn a new song using notation
- To learn and perform new songs
- To sing songs with attention to technique and expression

WHAT IS GOING TO HAPPEN?

- Children read and sing examples of melody written with rhythm sol-fa notation
- Singing songs with an appropriate sound, style and expression

SONGS

For phrases to be read, notated and performed

- Apple tree [page 108]
- I like coffee, I like tea [page 131]
- Rocky mountain [page 145]

Songs for expressive singing

- Ferry me across the water [page 119]
- Now the day is over [page 135]
- Rise, sun, awaken [page 144]

HOT SONG

- Pupils' requests

LISTENING

- Snow in Kalamazoo - Terpstra [track 103]

GENERAL GUIDANCE

To read and notate music is part of the ongoing acquisition of useful skills for a musician and is one of the aims of this progressive learning programme, **Inside Music**. Reading notation provides part of the road to musical independence. It does not restrict, but gives access and freedom of choice.

Rhythm sol-fa is only one of several accepted notations available to the musician. It is a vocal based notation, but will later make direct connections to staff notation for both voices and instruments.

Beauty is usually considered to be a subjective quality and yet, there is more common agreement about what is recognised as being 'beautiful' than we might realise. If it is possible to lay aside the biases and indeed, prejudices, about styles of music, one suspects that most people will recognise and acknowledge the beauty of sound, especially from the Singing Voice. Most importantly, we offer children the keys to unlocking the potential of their voice by introducing them to the some of the basic technical considerations of singing.

Published by The Voices Foundation and Alfred Publishing Co
© The Voices Foundation 2014

SET ONE Learning a new song via notation

The intention is to teach a new song with the help of known notation.

The 'Rocky Mountain' song melody is to be found in rhythm sol-fa notation in Song Melodies on page 172.

It is a deliberate intention, first to learn the *refrain*, ie phrases 3 and 4

Teaching the song 'Rocky Mountain'

- Class listens to the recording several times to give an aural picture of what is going to be learned

- Display phrase 3:

- Class reads, speaks and taps the rhythm notation of phrase 3

- To 'tune up', establish a pitch for **doh**, then sing and sign: **doh me soh lah**, followed by **me ray doh**

- Class now reads and sings phrase 3 several times

If it is helpful, play the song recording to check phrase 3

- Display phrase 4:

- Class reads and sings phrase 4

Have the pitch differences between the final notes of phrases 3 and 4 been recognised?

- Class reads and sings the refrain melody [phrases 3 and 4]

Again, if helpful, check with the recording

- Once secured, class sings the refrain to song words

Now phrases 1 and 2 [the verse melody], are tackled in the same way

Display phrase 1:

Display phrase 2:

- The whole song melody is read and sung to sol-fa singing names

- Finally, the song is sung to the song's words

SET TWO New songs

Teach the song 'Ferry me across the water'

'Ferry me across the water' is a very short theatre piece between two characters. There are two more verses of dialogue in the The Song pages.

- Once the complete song is known, two groups sing the roles of the characters, the ferryman and the passenger

- Pairs of children simultaneously rehearse the scene; they should consider characterisation and how that might be expressed through their singing and acting

- Two singers act out the scene for the 'audience' to watch and applaud

This is a traditional song of the Pawnee nation in USA. As the bringer of light, warmth and growth of food, the sun held a particular importance in the life of the Pawnee people for centuries.

- The singing should have regard to the spiritual nature of the words and the ritual that is being enacted at dawn

- What tempo will help to express this?

- What dynamics?

- Will the singing aim for a *legato* or *non-legato* style?

- What will be the colour of the singing tone? Dark/ Bright?

- Is there a role for a leader?

- How many times will the chant be sung?

- What do the words and melody suggest for the singing and performance?

- Consider an arrangement of several 'verses' that might involve humming and 'ah-ing' or other wordless vowels

- Consider singing style, tempo, dynamics

- Consider using individual voices or groups of voices

- Consider posture and breathing that supports the Singing Voice

- Perhaps children would like to add another verse that reflects the theme of twilight and evening time.

SET THREE Listening to unusual music

Listen to 'Snow in Kalamazoo'

This piece written by Koos Terpstra is for three percussion performers playing a mixture of marimba, conga drums, woodblocks and small gongs. Kalamazoo is a skiing resort in USA. The piece is meant to be impressionistic and has no literal intentions.

- Ask the children to listen and afterwards say what they can about the type of instruments they think are being played

LEARNING OUTCOMES

- Children can learn new music with the help of notation

- Children can apply technical knowledge and experience to performance

Published by The Voices Foundation and Alfred Publishing Co
© The Voices Foundation 2014

FOCUS

- Singing Development
- Performing: singing and playing
- Concepts: pitch, dynamics, tempo, phrase, rhythm, pulse
- Notation

TEACHING OBJECTIVES

- To reinforce and assess the skills, knowledge and understanding in the areas of singing development, performing, listening, notation and concepts, acquired during the teaching of Units 13 - 22

WHAT IS GOING TO HAPPEN?

- Activities are used that allow the class and individuals to demonstrate their skills, knowledge and understanding

SONGS

Using songs as listed under the different Teaching Ideas headings

HOT SONG

LISTENING

The Dargason - Holst [track 104]

GENERAL GUIDANCE

This second Revision Unit provides an opportunity for the children to revisit and reinforce some of the skills and knowledge they have encountered during *First Steps*. It is also a moment when the teacher can assess how well these developments have been assimilated by the children. It is time to take stock before moving on with the *Inside Music* programme.

The teacher is sometimes given repertoire options. Select songs with which the children are really familiar.

The assessment criteria head each section in the form of questions to the teacher.

IMPORTANT! The teacher can choose to use all the activities or as few as is necessary to demonstrate the children's competences and is helpful revision for the children.

Published by The Voices Foundation and Alfred Publishing Co
© The Voices Foundation 2014

Singing Voice

Assessing:

Do they continue to demonstrate a supportive posture when standing or sitting?

Do the children continue to breathe easily and sing with one breath per phrase?

Does the singing sound in tune?

Are children aware of how the shaping of the vowels affects the tone colour of their singing sound?

Can the sound be described as pleasing to the ear?

When called for, can they sing with a legato style?

Do the children sing with regard for the words, their meaning and character of the song using appropriate tempo, dynamics, singing style and expression?

Select one of the these songs known to the class:

- Heno, heno, hen blant bach [page 123]
- Hill an' gully ride-a [page 127]
- Ferry me across the water [page 119]

- Class stands to sing the song with 'best voices'
- Class sits to sing the song showing you a 'good' sitting posture
- Class sings demonstrating ease when taking a breath for each new phrase
- Two groups or individuals: one group sings the song; the other notes the starting pitch given by teacher or a group leader and listens to see if the song has been sung in tune and in their opinion has ended with exactly the pitch with which it started
- In discussion with the teacher, the class agrees on how to sing the selected song [style, tempo, dynamics, etc.]; in two groups, one performs to the other with a leader to set the pitch and tempo with *"Off you go!"* The listening group comments on the group's success.

Two-part Singing Voice

Assessing:

Can children sing as part of a group within a two-part piece?

Can children hold a drone securely while others sing the melody part?

Can children maintain a melodic ostinato part?

These songs should first be familiar to the class:

- Bells in the steeple
- Rocky mountain

- Two groups: one sings the song 'Bells in the steeple' as the other maintains a drone on the first note [**doh**], thus:

Ding_____dong_____throughout

- As above, but with the two individuals or two small groups
- Two-groups: one sings the song 'Rocky mountain' as the other maintains this melodic *ostinato*, repeated throughout:

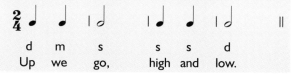

d	m	s	s	s	d
Up	we	go,	high	and	low.

Published by The Voices Foundation and Alfred Publishing Co
© The Voices Foundation 2014

Instrument playing

Are instruments known by their proper names?

Are instruments respected and cared for?

Do the relative heights of player and a tuned percussion instrument facilitate the use of beaters [mallets]?

Can children play pitch [tuned] percussion using two beaters?

Can children play song phrases on pitch percussion?

- Several children are asked to bring forward several pitch [tuned] percussion instruments and pairs of beaters, named by the teacher

- They report on the conditions in which they found the instruments

- Do they bring forward the asked-for instruments?

Select a song:

- John the blacksmith [page 134] Tone-set: l-s-m

  Melody starts on **soh**: suggest A lah, G soh, E me

- One for the mouse [page 138] Tone-set: m-r-d

  Melody starts on **me**: suggest A me, G ray, F doh

- Row, boat, row [page 146] Tone-set: l-s-m

  Melody starts on **soh**: suggest A lah, G soh, E me

- Suo gân [page 152] Tone-set: m-r-d

  Melody starts on **me**: suggest A me, G ray, F doh

- Class sings the song; sings to singing names; sings to instrument letter names

- Individuals play a phrase or phrases on pitch percussion as the rest play on 'finger bars' [see Units 19 and 21]

Listening to recorded music

Can the children listen with a given focus?

Can they use their knowledge about instruments, voices, phrase structure, pitch, rhythm, dynamics and tempo to talk about what they hear?

Listen to the 'Dargason'

This is an arrangement for a string orchestra by Gustav Holst of a 16th century folk dance tune. The Dargason tune heard at the opening is played repeatedly throughout this fast and furious piece, rather in the manner of a melodic *ostinato*. It is embellished with lots of other melodic motifs and includes the famous 'Greensleeves' melody, another 16th century tune.

- Ask the children to listen and say what they can about the opening tune and the piece in general:

  - What type of instrument is playing? [strings: violins, violas, cellos, basses]

  - What happened to the pitch of the dance tune? [it appeared among the lower sounding instruments sometimes]

  - Did the dance tune ever stop? [No]

  - Could anyone hear a different tune appear sometimes and can they describe it? [graceful, like a song]

  - How fast was the tempo? [fast!]

  - What dynamics were used? [quieter; louder]

- If appropriate, let the children hear the piece several times before and after discussion

Concept: pitch

Assessing:

*Can the children work aurally with the sol-fa singing names: **lah soh me ray doh** supported by the handsigns?*

Can they identify the sol-fa singing names used in song melody?

Do they know what a tone-set is?

From the following:

- Bounce high, bounce low [page 109] Tone-set: l-s-m

- Bells in the steeple [page 109] Tone-set: s-m-d

- Suo gân [page 152] Tone-set: m-r-d

- Ask the class to sing the song

- Tell them the first singing name and ask them to perform the song to sol-fa with supporting handsigns

- Ask individuals to perform

- What are the singing names used in the song and what is therefore the tone-set?

Concept: rhythm

Assessing:

Can the children work aurally with the speaking names for a crotchet [quarter] and its silent rest, pairs of quavers [eighths] and the minim [half]

Can they identify the rhythms used in a song phrase?

From the following:

- Row, boat, row [page 146] Phrases 1 and 2

- Plainie clappie [page 142] Phrases 1 and 2

- Hot cross buns [page 127] Phrases 1 and 2

- Ask the children to sing the song and to mark the pulse

- They tap the rhythm of phrase 1

- They tap and speak the rhythm names, touching the shoulders when a *rest* occurs, as in 'Row boat row'

- Ask individuals to perform

- Then move onto phrase 2

Notation: reading and writing

Assessing:

Can the children read and notate rhythm sol-fa using the elements listed under Concepts above?

Can they read and notate music that uses time signatures and bar lines?

Can the children explain what rhythm sol-fa is?

Can they describe what time signatures and bar lines are?

Display:

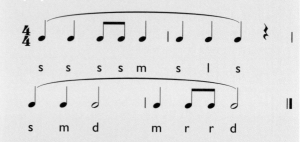

- Work with phrase 1 only

- To a given tempo, ask the class to tap the rhythm and 'speak' the rhythm names with the Thinking Voice

- To a given starting pitch, ask the class to 'sing' with the Thinking Voice and use handsigns

- Ask the class to sing phrase 1 to sol-fa singing names

- Ask individuals to sing the phrase

- Work with phrase 2 using the above procedure

- Ask the class to sing both phrases

Published by The Voices Foundation and Alfred Publishing Co
© The Voices Foundation 2014

Using pencil and paper and a board, the children are asked to notate the following [do not display]:

s l s   s m r d

- Tell the class what is going to happen

- Ask the children to write a $\frac{4}{4}$ time signature on their paper

- Phrase 1 only

- Establish a tempo and tap the rhythm, remembering to tap the minim in the manner suggested in Unit 20

- The class taps and speaks with rhythm names [**ta ta ta - a**]

- If helpful, repeat

- The class notates; check that all have drawn the correct rhythm

- You <u>hum</u> the pitch of the phrase; children copy; if helpful, repeat

- You tell the class that the first note is **soh**; they sing to singing names

- They write the letter names under the rhythm

- The complete notation is read and sung

- Ask the class to draw a phrase mark and to insert a new bar line

- Move onto phrase 2 and use the same procedure

Phrase structure

Assessing:

Can children aurally identify and label the phrases in a known song?

Can children look at notation with phrase marks and label the structure?

First sing the song 'Cock-Cock what is that'

- Children sing the song showing the phrases with hands 'drawing in the air' phrase marks; they are asked to draw on paper each of these in succession [4]

- Class is asked to identify the phrases as same or different and label them accordingly [A B A B]

Display the following and ask the class to write down the labels for the phrase structure [A B A C]

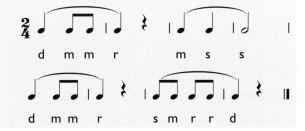

d m m r   m s   s

d m m r   s m r r d

Improvising and composing

Assessing:

Can the children improvise without then notating?

Can the children improvise and then notate as a composition?

The class is given a 4-beat 'refrain' rhythm phrase for all to tap

- A series of 4-beat improvised phrases are played on untuned percussion instruments after each refrain

For example:

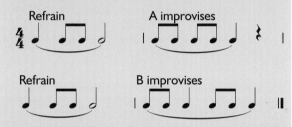

.....and so on

The children are asked to use their Thinking Voices to improvise 4-beat rhythm phrases; they are asked to choose their own phrase structure, perhaps, A A B C; once they have tapped and used rhythm names for their first phrase, they should notate it

- They improvise each new phrase; they notate all the phrases and insert phrase marks

- The rhythm pieces can be left as such and played on untuned percussion

- However, the composer may choose to turn the rhythm into a melody by adding sol-fa singing names; insist that the pitch should be improvised with the help of the Thinking Voice, using a tone-set of the composer's choosing; the composer must be able to sing the final melody and may afterwards play it on a pitch percussion instrument

Published by The Voices Foundation and Alfred Publishing Co
© The Voices Foundation 2014

The Songs

Song Index

Published by The Voices Foundation and Alfred Publishing Co
© The Voices Foundation 2014

Acha bacha

TYPE: CHOOSING GAME	TONESET: CHANT	TRACK: I

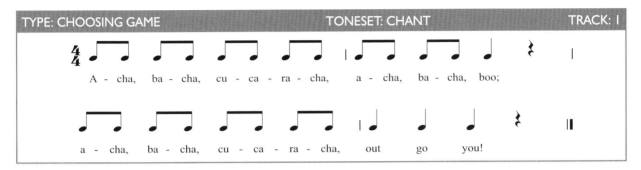

A - cha, ba - cha, cu - ca - ra - cha, a - cha, ba - cha, boo;

a - cha, ba - cha, cu - ca - ra - cha, out go you!

DESCRIPTION OF GAME, ACTION OR ACTIVITY

Children have traditionally used this rhyme to select a person who is going to be 'it' in a game to follow.

The rhyme can be used to bring about an awareness of the two 'rests'.

The children stand in a circle but as pairs facing each other. With each beat of the rhyme, each person:

> **slaps** own knees
> **claps** own hands
> **slaps** right-to-right-hand with partner
> **slaps** left-to-left-hand with partner
> **claps** own hands
> **slaps both hands** with the corresponding hands of the partner
> **jumps round** at the first 'rest' to face the pupil behind

This sequence is repeated for the second phrase.

For variation set a series of different speeds [tempos] including slow. To establish the tempo play four preliminary beats on an instrument. Teacher, pupil or pupils can adjudicate how well the tempo was maintained and how well the actions were performed with the pulse.

Allundé alluya

TYPE: SWAHILI LULLABY	TONESET: d'-l-s-m-r-d	TRACK: 2

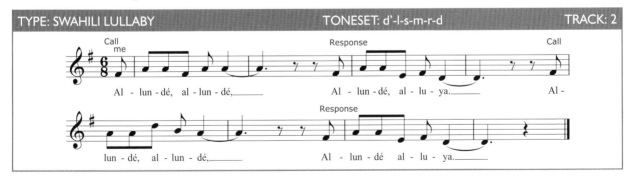

Call me / Response / Call

Al - lun - dé, al - lun - dé,_____ Al - lun - dé, al - lu - ya._____ Al -

lun - dé, al - lun - dé,_____ Al - lun - dé al - lu - ya._____

DESCRIPTION OF GAME, ACTION OR ACTIVITY

This is part of a traditional prayer lullaby from the Swahili-speaking people of East Africa. The full prayer asks for the god of the sunrise to protect the child, help the infant to grow and become a worthy member of the tribe.

Teacher and class can perform the song singing alternate phrases, or alternatively it can be performed by two groups or two children.

Published by The Voices Foundation and Alfred Publishing Co
© The Voices Foundation 2014

Apple tree

TYPE: CHOOSING GAME   TONESET: l-s-m   TRACK: 3

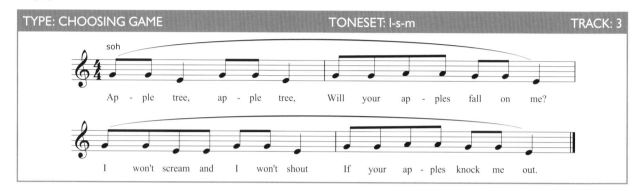

Ap - ple tree, ap - ple tree, Will your ap - ples fall on me?

I won't scream and I won't shout If your ap - ples knock me out.

DESCRIPTION OF GAME, ACTION OR ACTIVITY

The children in pairs, face to face, form a circle. Several pairs, equidistant to each other, make an arch with raised arms and joined hands. As everyone sings, the other pairs move in the same direction through the arches. On reaching the last word, the arches drop their arms to 'capture' the couple passing through at that moment. The 'captured' pair now join the 'arch' pairs by standing behind them. After the circle has been 'shrunk', repeat the song and activity several times. The last couples to be captured become the next 'arches'. The game is probably best played with two circles performing simultaneously.

Baby 123

TYPE: ACTION SONG   TONESET: ma-r-d-l,s,   TRACK: 4

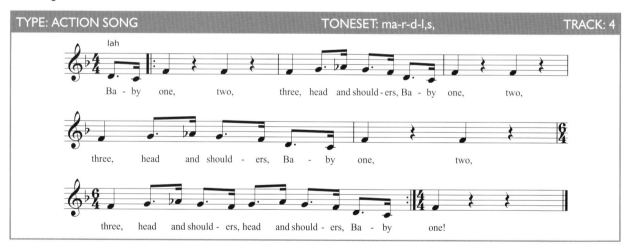

Ba - by one, two, three, head and should - ers, Ba - by one, two,

three, head and should - ers, Ba - by one, two,

three, head and should - ers, head and should - ers, Ba - by one!

DESCRIPTION OF GAME, ACTION OR ACTIVITY

The children make a circle.

This song works its way, with actions, down the various parts of the body.

1. Head and shoulders
2. Shoulders elbows
3. Elbows hips
4. Hips and knees
5. Knees and toes

At the end of the last verse all the parts should be recapped as follows:

Knees and toes and hips and knees and elbows hips and shoulders elbows head and shoulders, baby one!

Once the song is well known gentle finger clicks can be inserted after 'one' and 'two'.

Published by The Voices Foundation and Alfred Publishing Co
© The Voices Foundation 2014

Bells in the steeple

TYPE: SWEDISH MELODY   TONESET: s-m-d   TRACK: 5

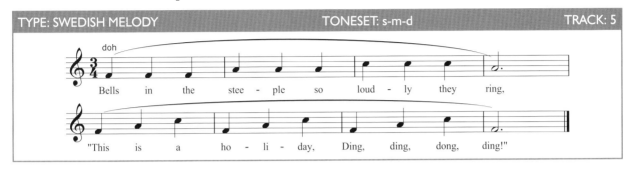

DESCRIPTION OF GAME, ACTION OR ACTIVITY

Ask the children to stand in a circle and to place the left hand slightly forward, palm facing up. Singing at a steady tempo, the right hand gently taps on the left palm for one beat and then taps two beats on the palm of the neighbour on the right. This pattern of three actions is repeated to the end of the song and illustrates the metre of 3: **strong** – weak – weak.

The class stands as a circle with each third child holding a pair of claves/sticks. As the song is sung, the children with the instruments play once for the first of the three beats. The child to the immediate right taps on the palm of one hand for the second beat and the next to the right taps the third beat. Meanwhile all the pupils with claves/sticks move outside the circle and walk anti-clockwise into the first space vacated and in time to play the next first beat of three. The sequence is repeated and maintained throughout the song. It is advised that a slow tempo is used initially.

Bounce high, bounce low

TYPE: NAMING GAME   TONESET: l-s-m   TRACK: 6

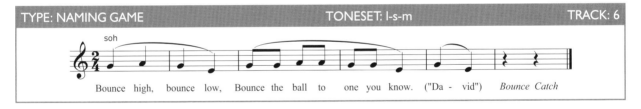

DESCRIPTION OF GAME, ACTION OR ACTIVITY

The class forms a circle, with one child in the centre holding a medium-size ball. This person bounces the ball each time the word 'bounce' is sung. The child selects the next person by singing his or her name at the end. The ball is immediately bounced to the new child who goes with the ball to the centre and the game is repeated.

Singing Development: When singing the chosen name, the solo singer should pitch-match with the rest of the class.

Bow wow wow

TYPE: ACTION SONG	TONESET: l-s-m-r-d	TRACK: 7

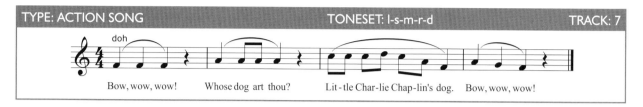

DESCRIPTION OF GAME, ACTION OR ACTIVITY

Standing in a circle, each child faces a partner and performs actions as follows:

Bow, wow, wow — With both hands held at about shoulder height and palms facing forward, the partners slap each other's hands three times to the pulse ('high five' style).

Whose dog art thou? — Each child points and wags a finger to the pulse.

Little Charlie Chaplin's dog — The partners swing each other with linked arms or hands so as to exchange places.

Bow, wow, wow — The partners slap hands three times in 'high five' style as before and then immediately jump and spin round on the spot. Each child now faces a new partner and the game can begin again.

Brown bread and butter O

TYPE: NAMING SONG	TONESET: l-s-f-m-r-d	TRACK: 8

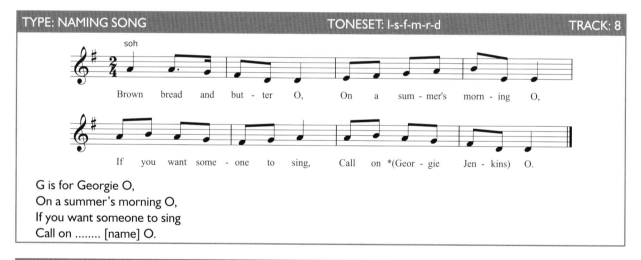

G is for Georgie O,
On a summer's morning O,
If you want someone to sing
Call on .... [name] O.

DESCRIPTION OF GAME, ACTION OR ACTIVITY

The children perform up to, and including, the word 'sing', where a pre-selected child sings 'Call on .... O' with the first and last names of another pupil, eg 'Call on Peter Goddard O'. The second verse immediately follows with the initial letter and the first name of the selected pupil. That child will sing from 'Call on ....', thus providing the names of the next person. The challenge is never to miss a beat and not to repeat any previous names.

After a certain number of repetitions, the song could be concluded and children asked to remember if they were NOT named for the next occasion.

Published by The Voices Foundation and Alfred Publishing Co

Bubblegum, bubblegum

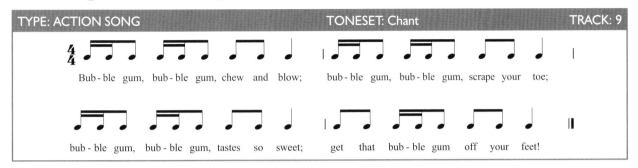

| TYPE: ACTION SONG | TONESET: Chant | TRACK: 9 |

Bub-ble gum, bub-ble gum, chew and blow; bub-ble gum, bub-ble gum, scrape your toe;

bub-ble gum, bub-ble gum, tastes so sweet; get that bub-ble gum off your feet!

DESCRIPTION OF GAME, ACTION OR ACTIVITY

Standing in a circle all the children say the words as they do the actions in time to the rhythm:

First three phrases

Bubblegum, bubblegum - tap right knee, left knee, clap hands

Chew and blow / scrape your toe / tastes so sweet - tap alternate shoulders twice and then head once

Fourth phrase

Get that - tap shoulders twice

Bubblegum - tap right knee, left knee, clap hands

Off your feet - tap alternate shoulders twice and then head once

Taken from Singing Games and Rhymes for Middle Years by Lucinda Geoghegan
Printed by the National Youth Choir of Scotland www.nycos.co.uk

Published by The Voices Foundation and Alfred Publishing Co

Button you must wander

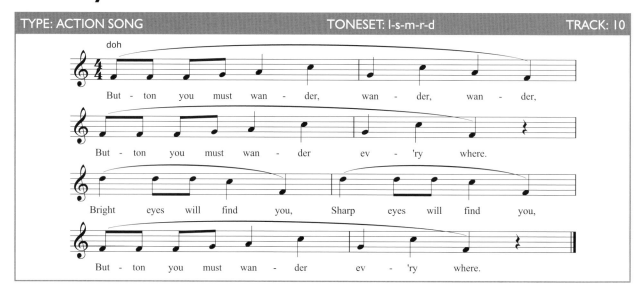

TYPE: ACTION SONG TONESET: l-s-m-r-d TRACK: 10

But - ton you must wan - der, wan - der, wan - der,

But - ton you must wan - der ev - 'ry where.

Bright eyes will find you, Sharp eyes will find you,

But - ton you must wan - der ev - 'ry where.

DESCRIPTION OF GAME, ACTION OR ACTIVITY

The children stand in a circle with both hands outstretched in front, the back of each hand uppermost, holding on to a loop of string which goes round the entire circle. During the singing of the song, a button (or similar) that has been threaded onto the string is passed covertly from hand to hand round the circle. A child standing in the centre tries to detect who has the button at the end of the song.

Singing Development: The children need to approach the singing of the third phrase with an awareness of 'high' thinking, a 'tall' posture and lots of tummy muscle support.

Published by The Voices Foundation and Alfred Publishing Co
© The Voices Foundation 2014

Can you tap this rhythm?

| TYPE: ACTION SONG | TONESET: s-m-d | TRACK: 11 |

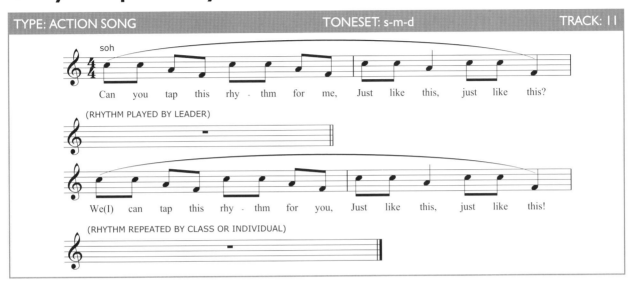

DESCRIPTION OF GAME, ACTION OR ACTIVITY

The leader of the game sings the question followed by a 4-beat improvised rhythm phrase within the same tempo. The class [or group or individual] either:

> immediately responds by copying the given rhythm and then sings phrase 2

or:

> sings phrase 2 first and then performs the rhythm phrase - this is much more challenging

Additional listening and thinking skills can be added to the game, for example:

> the leader performs the phrase with consciously considered dynamics that the class must replicate; if the leader considers the phrase has not been replicated accurately then, without saying why, he/she immediately performs the same phrase once more for the class to try again.

Che che kule

TYPE: ACTION SONG   **TONESET: d-l-s**   **TRACK: 12**

DESCRIPTION OF GAME, ACTION OR ACTIVITY

This is an echo and action song from Ghana.

1. Each phrase is sung by a leader and imitated by the class. The leader simultaneously performs a strong action (eg tapping shoulders) for each pulse and the class also copies this.

2. When pupils have some experience in leading the game, they can be encouraged to change to another action at some point during the performance.

3. Experienced leaders can be encouraged to change the action for each new phrase, perhaps over several repeats of the song. The leader's invention should always be regulated by considerations of practicality, safety, maintaining a steady pulse and quality of singing.

Chest, chest, knee, toe

TYPE: ACTION SONG   **TONESET: l-s-m-r-d**   **TRACK: 13**

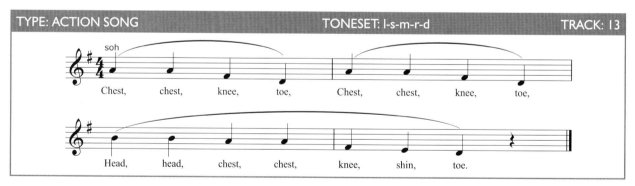

DESCRIPTION OF GAME, ACTION OR ACTIVITY

The class stands to sing and as they do so, they tap the part of the body indicated by the words.

Published by The Voices Foundation and Alfred Publishing Co
© The Voices Foundation 2014

Chicken on a fence post

TYPE: USA FOLKSONG GAME   TONESET: l-s-m-r-d-l,-s,   TRACK: 14

DESCRIPTION OF GAME, ACTION OR ACTIVITY

The children stand in a circle. One child, the Chicken, is in the centre of the circle. He is blindfold and holds out a hand. Everyone sings phrases 1 – 3 and walks around him in a circle. Meanwhile, another child is chosen to go into the circle and shake the hand of the Chicken whilst singing the last phrase, using the name of the Chicken in place of 'Susie Brown'. The Chicken guesses who this is.

Coca-Cola went to town

TYPE: CHILDREN'S RHYME   TONESET: l-s-m-r-d   TRACK: 15

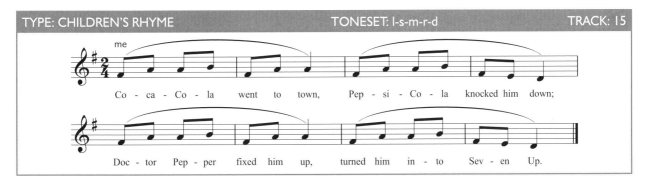

DESCRIPTION OF GAME, ACTION OR ACTIVITY

This is a rhyme with many variations and added verses by children on both sides of the Atlantic Ocean. It is the custom of playground rhymes that variants of the original source will evolve. The children may wish to create new words, perhaps about cartoon characters or jungle animals.

The class could devise 'clap-and-slap' action sequences with a partner or in small groups, which are performed as they sing the rhyme.

When a class presents playground songs with their actions to other pupils in a school assembly, it can have the effect of 'catching-on'; this is an effective way of teaching new songs to others.

Ding, dong, I've got the rhythm

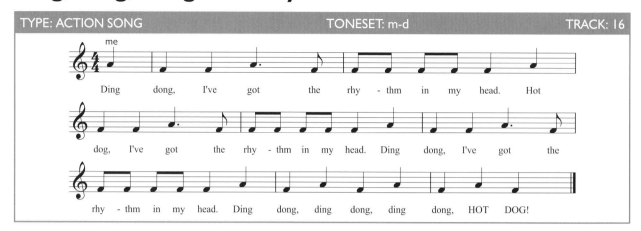

| TYPE: ACTION SONG | TONESET: m-d | TRACK: 16 |

DESCRIPTION OF GAME, ACTION OR ACTIVITY

The children stand in pairs, facing each other.

For each 'Ding dong!', the children move their heads from side to side

For each 'I've got the rhythm in my head', the children tap the rhythm of the words on their hands

For each 'Hot dog!', they slap both hands with those of their partner, twice.

When experience has been gained, the song with actions could be sung, but using the Thinking

Voice for each 'Hot dog' or, on another occasion, 'I've got the rhythm in my head'.

Doggie, doggie

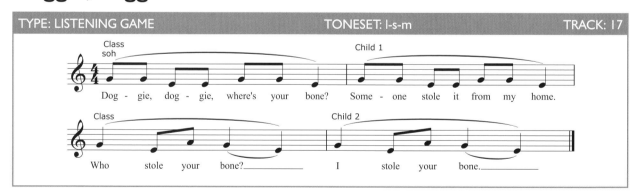

| TYPE: LISTENING GAME | TONESET: l-s-m | TRACK: 17 |

DESCRIPTION OF GAME, ACTION OR ACTIVITY

The children sit in a circle. A child is invited to be the 'doggie' and sits in the 'kennel' in the centre of the circle – or elsewhere – but unable to see the children in the circle. Another child is quietly chosen to hold the 'bone' and to conceal it.

The class sings the first phrase and the 'doggie' replies. The class sings the third phrase and the child holding the 'bone' responds. By listening carefully to the Singing Voice, the 'doggie' identifies the child who has the bone.

If the children find this activity too easy, the child with the 'bone' might be asked to disguise her Singing Voice. A further challenge for the 'doggie' would be to employ two bones, with the 'bone' children singing their responses simultaneously.

Singing Challenge: The 'doggie' and 'bone' children should be expected to pitch-match the rest of the singing, even when trying to disguise their voices.

Published by The Voices Foundation and Alfred Publishing Co
© The Voices Foundation 2014

Double, double

TYPE: ACTION RHYME   **TONESET: Chant**   **TRACK: 18**

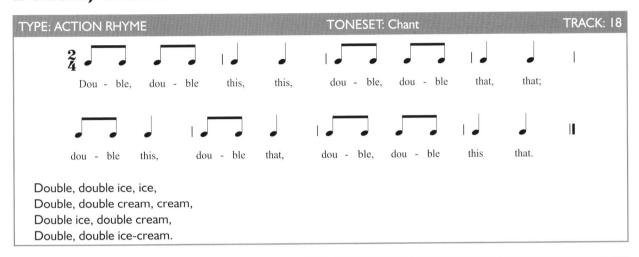

Dou - ble, dou - ble this, this, dou - ble, dou - ble that, that;

dou - ble this, dou - ble that, dou - ble, dou - ble this that.

Double, double ice, ice,
Double, double cream, cream,
Double ice, double cream,
Double, double ice-cream.

DESCRIPTION OF GAME, ACTION OR ACTIVITY

This game is played with partners facing each other. Both hold up their fists, keeping thumbs towards their own face. All movements are to the pulse, as follows:

Double, double	Both gently touch fists
This, this.	Both gently touch palms of hands
Double, double	Both gently touch fists
That, that.	Both gently touch backs of hands
Double this,	Fist, palms
Double that,	Fist, backs
Double, double	Both gently touch fists
This, that.	Palms, backs.

The tempo of the chant might be changed to practise control of faster and slower speeds.

Children could invent new verses by simply finding two related words of a single syllable each, such as 'fish-cake' or, one word of two syllables such as 'pa-per' and splitting the syllables. So, for example:

'Double, double fish, fish,
Double, double cake, cake...'

'Double, double pa(y), pa(y),
Double, double per, per...'

Published by The Voices Foundation and Alfred Publishing Co
© The Voices Foundation 2014

Down by the ocean

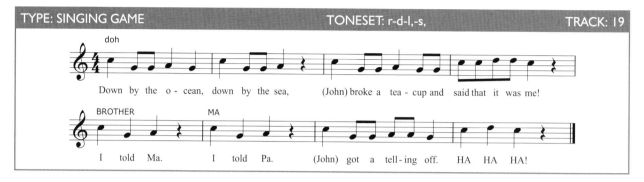

TYPE: SINGING GAME   **TONESET: r-d-l,-s,**   **TRACK: 19**

Down by the o-cean, down by the sea, (John) broke a tea-cup and said that it was me!

I told Ma. I told Pa. (John) got a tell-ing off. HA HA HA!

DESCRIPTION OF GAME, ACTION OR ACTIVITY

The children form a circle and one of them is selected to be in the centre. This person is blindfolded and his/her first name is used appropriately in the song – see the brackets.

During the early part of the singing the teacher silently selects two other pupils to sing the parts of BROTHER/ SISTER and MA. At the end of the song the blindfolded child must say who sang the solo parts.

Engine, engine

TYPE: SONG   **TONESET: : l-s-m-r-d**   **TRACK: 20**

En - gine, en - gine, num - ber nine, Run - ning on the Lon - don line.

If she's pol - ished, how she'll shine, En - gine, en - gine, num - ber nine.

2. Engine, engine, number nine,
   Running on the Glasgow line,
   Through the mountains looking fine,
   Engine, engine, number nine.

3. Engine, engine, number nine,
   Running on the Swansea line,
   Bringing coal back from the mine,
   Engine, engine, number nine.

DESCRIPTION OF GAME, ACTION OR ACTIVITY

Show the children that this melody has four equal-length phrases. By agreement in advance, the 'train' sings the song with Singing Voices, except for phrase 2 when the children use their Thinking Voices as though the train had gone into a tunnel. In this way, other phrases might be used as 'tunnel phrases'. For example, a very long tunnel might need two, or more, phrases. The challenge is to maintain a steady tempo when using Thinking Voices so that the singers emerge from the tunnel-phrases at the same time! The tempo could be varied for each new performance to suit the new speed of the 'train'.

Published by The Voices Foundation and Alfred Publishing Co

Ev'ryone, good morning

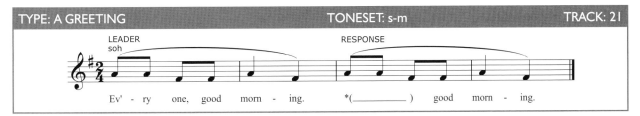

| TYPE: A GREETING | TONESET: s-m | TRACK: 21 |

DESCRIPTION OF GAME, ACTION OR ACTIVITY

This introductory greeting is a great way to start the day or a lesson.

Ferry me across the water

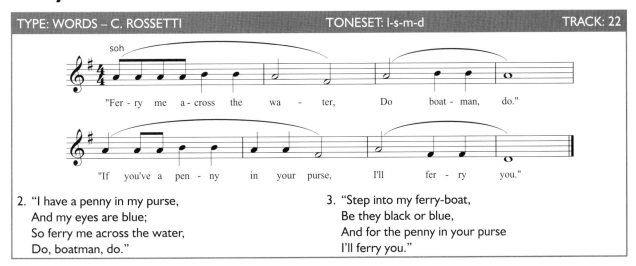

| TYPE: WORDS – C. ROSSETTI | TONESET: l-s-m-d | TRACK: 22 |

2. "I have a penny in my purse,
   And my eyes are blue;
   So ferry me across the water,
   Do, boatman, do."

3. "Step into my ferry-boat,
   Be they black or blue,
   And for the penny in your purse
   I'll ferry you."

DESCRIPTION OF GAME, ACTION OR ACTIVITY

The song can be performed by two groups of singers, or two soloists, each assuming the role of the passenger or the ferryman.

Published by The Voices Foundation and Alfred Publishing Co
© The Voices Foundation 2014

Fire! Fire!

TYPE: CHILDREN'S RHYME	TONESET: s-m	TRACK: 23

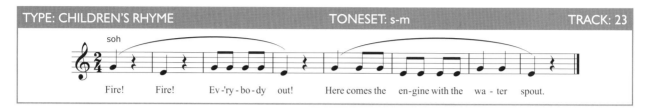

Fire! Fire! Ev-'ry-bo-dy out! Here comes the en-gine with the wa-ter spout.

DESCRIPTION OF GAME, ACTION OR ACTIVITY

In order to raise awareness of the music *rests*, the children sing the song and at each *rest* insert the sound of a squirt of water by emitting a *'sssh'*. The tempo must remain constant and the rhythm of the melody undisturbed. The tempo could be varied for each new performance in which case the rhythmic length of the *'sssh'* sound must be appropriate.

After several occasions the water sound *'dries up'* and each *rest* is 'filled' with 'dry' silence! In this way the impact of the *rest* as a silent rhythm feature is very telling.

Funga alafia

TYPE: SONG	TONESET: m-r-d-l,-s,-m,	TRACK: 24

Fun-ga a-la-fi-a, a-sche, a-sche Fun-ga a-la-fi-a, a-sche, a-sche

DESCRIPTION OF GAME, ACTION OR ACTIVITY

This is a traditional greeting song from Nigeria. It is in the Yoruba language and there are various translations of the words. Broadly it means 'welcome and blessings'.

It can be sung either as a call 'Funga alafia' and response 'asche, asche' or with everyone singing all of it.

There are many variations on the movements that can be used with the song [see YouTube].

Here is one version that involves singing the song 4 times:

Children stand in a circle:

1. In time to the pulse, move 4 steps to the left [left foot, together, 4x] and clap on the last pulse. Do the same starting with the right foot so that you end up where you started.

2. On the spot make a 'skiing' movement with the arms and the upper body - left 2x and then to the right 2x. Repeat movement

3. Tap forehead lightly 4 times and then extend arms in front of body with palms up and move 4 times. Tap mouth lightly 4 times and repeat the extended arms movement.

4. Finish by doing the first movement again.

Published by The Voices Foundation and Alfred Publishing Co

Goblins are around tonight

TYPE: SONG TONESET: m-r-d-t,-l, TRACK: 25

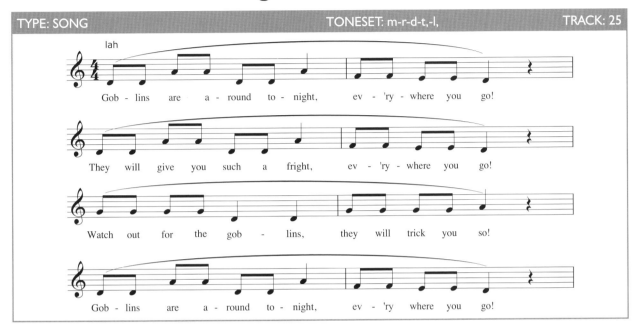

DESCRIPTION OF GAME, ACTION OR ACTIVITY

Children will enjoy the humour of changing the word 'Goblins' into 'Teachers'!

Singing Development: The words of the song suggest a very *legato* (unbroken sound) style of singing with one breath per phrase. The dynamics should be quiet – although the third phrase might suggest a slightly louder sound with a slight accent on 'watch out' and a 'sinister' *crescendo* (becoming louder) in the second half of the phrase. Return to a quieter sound with a continuous *diminuendo* (becoming quieter) for the final phrase.

Published by The Voices Foundation and Alfred Publishing Co
© The Voices Foundation 2014

Have you ever, ever?

TYPE: : UK ACTION SONG   TONESET: m-r-d   TRACK: 26

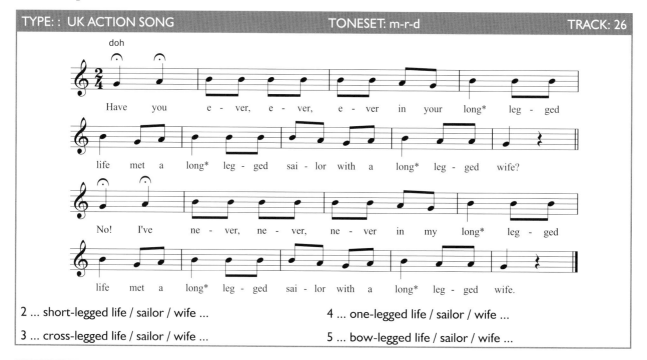

2 ... short-legged life / sailor / wife ...

3 ... cross-legged life / sailor / wife ...

4 ... one-legged life / sailor / wife ...

5 ... bow-legged life / sailor / wife ...

DESCRIPTION OF GAME, ACTION OR ACTIVITY

The children perform the following actions independently of each other. On the notes with pause signs they drum with fast alternating hand slaps on the knees; they then alternately slap with both hands on the knees and handclap to the pulse. For each 'long-legged' they show hands wide apart vertically to suggest 'long' followed by further alternating hand claps and knee-slaps. This sequence is repeated several times. In subsequent verses the hands and arms are appropriately used to suggest 'short-legged', 'cross-legged', 'one-legged' and 'bow-legged'.

For a different kind of experience, children are asked to sing and perform the actions, but on reaching each 'long-legged' it is 'sung' by the Thinking Voice.

Published by The Voices Foundation and Alfred Publishing Co
© The Voices Foundation 2014

Heno, heno, hen blant bach

TYPE: WELSH LULLABY　　　　　**TONESET: s-f-m-r-d**　　　　　**TRACK: 27**

He-no, he-no, hen blant bach,　　*He-no, he-no, hen blant bach,*

Di-me, di-me, di-me, hen blant bach,　　*Di-me, di-me, di-me, hen blant bach.*

2. Gwely, gwely, hen blant bach,
   Gwely, gwely, hen blant bach,
   Dime, dime, dime, hen blant bach,
   Dime, dime, dime, hen blant bach.

3. Fory, fory, hen blant bach,
   Fory, fory, hen blant bach,
   Dime, dime, dime, hen blant bach,
   Dime, dime, dime, hen blant bach.

Pronunciation:

heno = hair-nor; *hen blant bach* = hane blant barch; *dime* = dim-eh; *gwely* = gwe-lee; *fory* = vore-ee

DESCRIPTION OF GAME, ACTION OR ACTIVITY

This is a lullaby with several simple Welsh words. They have little meaning, but the purpose is to lull the little one to sleep.

English

1. Tonight, tonight, dear little children ...
   Halfpenny, halfpenny, halfpenny, dear little children ...

2. Bed, bed, dear little children ...
   Halfpenny, halfpenny, halfpenny, dear little children ...

3. Tomorrow, tomorrow, dear little children ...
   Halfpenny, halfpenny, halfpenny, dear little children ...

Here I come

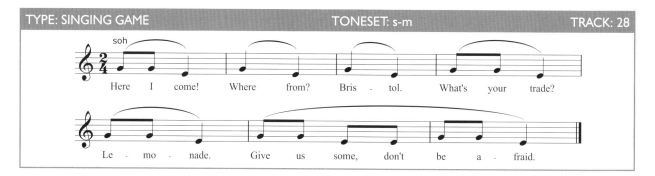

TYPE: SINGING GAME   **TONESET: s-m**   **TRACK: 28**

soh

Here I come! Where from? Bris - tol. What's your trade?

Le - mo - nade. Give us some, don't be a - fraid.

DESCRIPTION OF GAME, ACTION OR ACTIVITY

The leader sings, "Here I come"; the class responds, "Where from?" The song continues in this alternating style. At the end of the song, every child holds out an imaginary glass and the leader pretends to pour a drink into the glass of one outstretched hand – this selects the next leader and the game continues.

Singing Development: The leader sets the starting pitch, tempo and dynamics for the others to replicate. Encourage the leader to consider these before starting.

Here sits a fat cat

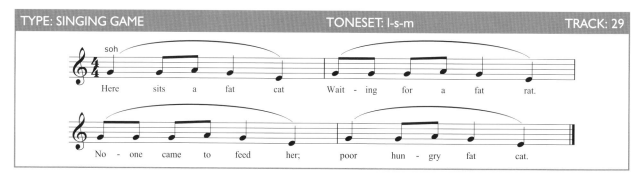

TYPE: SINGING GAME   **TONESET: l-s-m**   **TRACK: 29**

soh

Here sits a fat cat Wait - ing for a fat rat.

No - one came to feed her; poor hun - gry fat cat.

DESCRIPTION OF GAME, ACTION OR ACTIVITY

The children sit as a circle. One child is selected to be the 'fat cat' curled up in the middle of the circle, with closed eyes. A set of small bells, or similar, is placed behind the 'cat'. As the song is sung, a selected child creeps up and quietly takes the bells back to his place, hiding them from sight. At the end of the song the 'cat' has to guess who stole the bells.

Singing Development: The song is sung gently and quietly so as not to disturb the 'fat cat'.

Published by The Voices Foundation and Alfred Publishing Co

Hi! My name's Joe

TYPE: CUMULATIVE ACTIONS	TONESET: CHANT	TRACK: 30

Hi! My name's Joe.
I've got a wife and three kids and I work in a button factory.
One day the boss said, 'Joe, are you busy?'
I said, 'No',
So he said, 'Push the button with your * right hand'

* See the game description

DESCRIPTION OF GAME, ACTION OR ACTIVITY

This is a cumulative chant-game requiring a great deal of focus from the children.

The chant is performed in rap style and to a steady pulse tapped on an untuned percussion instrument. There are several repeats of the chant, each occasion adding on a new action.

The actions:

At the end of the first rap -

1. Right hand makes a windscreen wiper motion from left to right.
   This continues during the next verse

After the second rap add -

2. 'Left hand' - left hand joins the right hand

Then -

3. 'Right foot' - moves up and down

4. 'Left foot' - walking on the spot

5. 'Head' - head nod up and down

6. 'Tongue' - tongue sticks out and the next verse is 'said'!

To finish, chant -

One day the boss said, 'Joe, are you busy?'
I said, 'YES!'

Published by The Voices Foundation and Alfred Publishing Co
© The Voices Foundation 2014

High, low, chickalow

TYPE: PLAYGROUND ACTION SONG   TONESET: d'-l-s   TRACK: 31

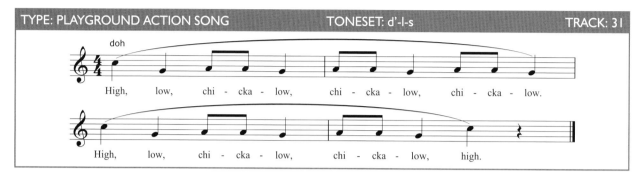

DESCRIPTION OF GAME, ACTION OR ACTIVITY

Working with a partner, the children extend their left hands and join them as if shaking hands. All movements are performed to the pulse.

On the word 'high' the right hands of each person clap above the joined left hands and below the joined hands for 'low': also for '-low' in 'chickalow'

On 'chicka' the right hand taps the back of the partner's left hand.

The tempo [not too fast] and pitch need to be established before starting the song; both of these can be changed for succeeding performances.

Variants:

The children repeat these actions, but this time using joined right hands.

As an alternative, still working with a partner, the children extend their left hands and place them back-to-back, rather than holding hands. The actions then proceed as before.

Published by The Voices Foundation and Alfred Publishing Co
© The Voices Foundation 2014

Hill an' gully ride-a

TYPE: JAMAICAN WORK SONG   TONESET: l-s-m-r-d-l,-s,   TRACK: 32

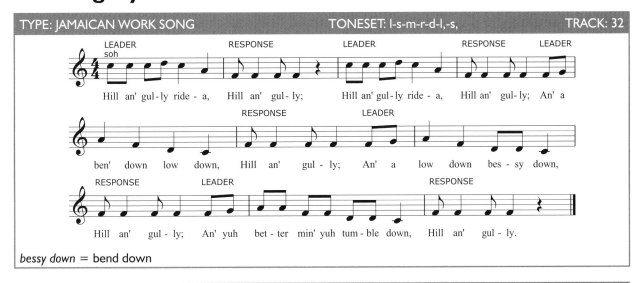

bessy down = bend down

DESCRIPTION OF GAME, ACTION OR ACTIVITY

This is a traditional call-and-response song from Jamaica and was sung by workmen constructing new roads. The words refer to the uneven and hazardous terrain through which the road had to be built. As the leader sang out his call, the pickaxes were raised for the downward swing. The first word of the response from the work gang was accompanied by the thud of the pickaxes as they struck the ground.

Hot cross buns

TYPE: UK STREET SELLER'S CRY   TONESET: s-f-m-r-d-s,   TRACK: 33

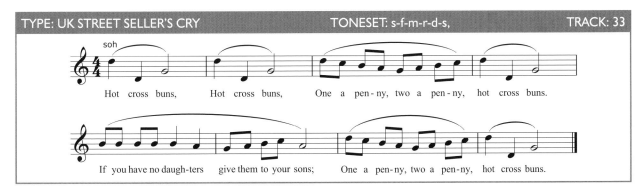

DESCRIPTION OF GAME, ACTION OR ACTIVITY

This traditional English street cry refers to the spiced buns associated with Good Friday.
There are references to hot cross buns as early as 1733 in the form of a ditty:
"Good Friday comes this month, the old woman runs,
With one or two a Penny hot cross Bunns."
The first published version of the present rhyme came in 1798.

Singing Development: In order to sing this song successfully it will be necessary to start at a higher pitch level so that the lower pitch on 'cross' can be reached by the pupils' voices. Be aware that wide leaps in the melody can cause some children to stretch the chin up for the high pitch sounds and pull the chin in to the throat for the low pitch sounds. Both of these movements cause voice production problems.

Published by The Voices Foundation and Alfred Publishing Co
© The Voices Foundation 2014

How many miles to Babylon?

TYPE: UK STREET GAME	TONESET: s-m-r-d	TRACK: 34

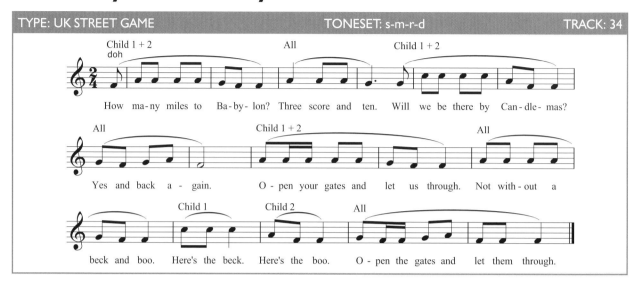

DESCRIPTION OF GAME, ACTION OR ACTIVITY

The children form two lines. The top couple turn and face down towards the other end of their line. They sing the questions and everyone else answers. At "Here's the beck", the first child throws his head and shoulders backwards and at "Here's the boo", the partner drops her head and shoulders forward. The lines form arches and the couple goes under to the other end. The game continues with the new top couple.

Published by The Voices Foundation and Alfred Publishing Co

I can take my tea

TYPE: ANGLO-AMERICAN GAME   TONESET: d'-l-s-m-r-d   TRACK: 35

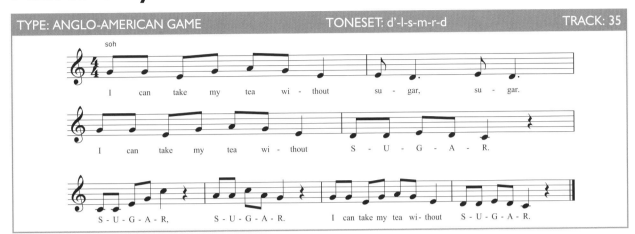

DESCRIPTION OF GAME, ACTION OR ACTIVITY

The song melody originally belonged to 'Camptown Races,' a minstrel song written in 1850 by the American, Stephen Foster. The famous Christy Minstrels, a group of travelling entertainers, first sang it.

The activity:

1. Pupils kneel in a circle, each with a rhythm stick or similar. Holding the stick in the right-hand, each pupil simultaneously places it in front of the person on his/her right to coincide with the first beat of the song.

2. The stick in front of each singer is picked up using the right hand on the 2nd beat, placed down in front of the person to the right on the 3rd beat and the 'new' stick picked up on the 4th.

3. Using this stick each pupil taps out the rhythm of 'sugar' on the floor. The game continues with each 'sugar' rhythm being tapped on the floor while sticks are moved on to the right for each 'I can take my tea without -'

When they are familiar with the songs and the game, a new challenge can be added. Select a letter from the word 'S-U-G-A-R' and, as the game is performed the pupils sing the letter using the Thinking Voice. The stick can still tap the letter but later try both singing the letter in the Thinking Voice and not tapping the stick.

I have lost the cupboard key

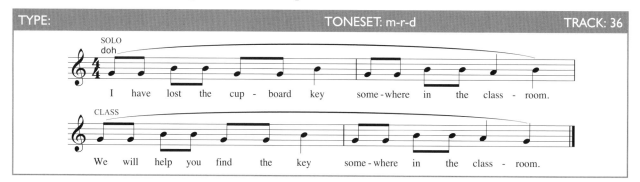

TYPE: **TONESET: m-r-d** **TRACK: 36**

SOLO
I have lost the cup-board key some-where in the class-room.

CLASS
We will help you find the key some-where in the class-room.

DESCRIPTION OF GAME, ACTION OR ACTIVITY

One child leaves the room and another then hides the key. The first child returns and is guided by the class in finding the key, singing the second phrase more quietly when she is far from the key and louder as she gets nearer to it. The song is repeated as often as is necessary for the 'seeker' to find the key or the search is abandoned.

Singing Development: The children are being asked to show vocal control and an ability to sing with variations of dynamic. They are asked not to lose their Singing Voices – that is, to avoid the extremes of whispering or shouting. For this activity it might be better if the class stands.

I heard, I heard

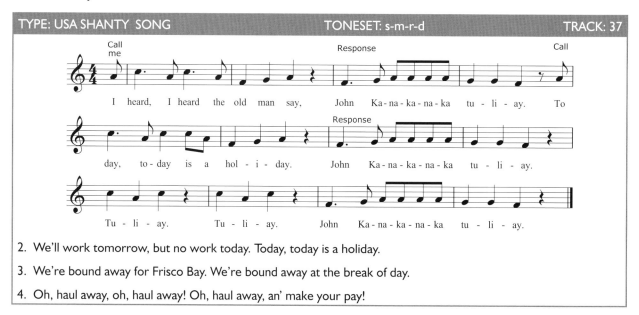

TYPE: USA SHANTY SONG **TONESET: s-m-r-d** **TRACK: 37**

Call
I heard, I heard the old man say, John Ka-na-ka-na-ka tu-li-ay. To

Response

Call

day, to-day is a hol-i-day. John Ka-na-ka-na-ka tu-li-ay.

Response

Tu-li-ay. Tu-li-ay. John Ka-na-ka-na-ka tu-li-ay.

2. We'll work tomorrow, but no work today. Today, today is a holiday.

3. We're bound away for Frisco Bay. We're bound away at the break of day.

4. Oh, haul away, oh, haul away! Oh, haul away, an' make your pay!

DESCRIPTION OF GAME, ACTION OR ACTIVITY

This is a typical shanty, a 'call-and-response' song. The shanty was often used as a work song for hauling ropes on a 19th century sailing ship. The leader – the shanty man – would improvise the words of the call, often at the expense of the officers of the ship when he thought he could not be heard by them!

Kanaka in Hawaiian means 'person'. The American trading ships of the Pacific Ocean employed many Kanakas who would work for several months of the year before returning with their earnings to Hawaii or other Polynesian islands.

Published by The Voices Foundation and Alfred Publishing Co
© The Voices Foundation 2014

I like coffee, I like tea

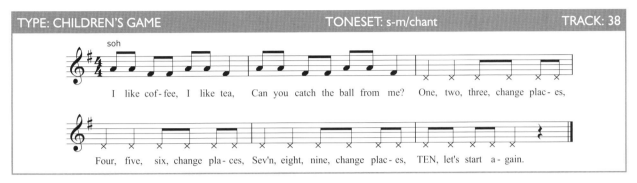

| TYPE: CHILDREN'S GAME | TONESET: s-m/chant | TRACK: 38 |

DESCRIPTION OF GAME, ACTION OR ACTIVITY

The pupils stand in a circle. The chosen leader goes into the centre with a ball. The leader bounces the ball to the feel of the pulse as everyone sings the first line. As the pupils chant the next part, the leader throws the ball to someone on 'one', it thrown back to him on 'two', and thrown again to someone else on 'three'; the leader and the latter person with the ball change places. The pattern is repeated for the remainder of the chant, except on 'ten' the ball is passed to someone who the goes into the middle to start the game again.

(The game for this song has been adapted by Lucinda Geoghegan)

I, I, me oh my [© 1977 by Boosey & Hawkes Music Publishers Ltd]

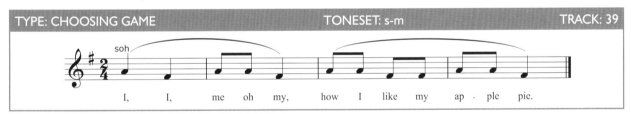

| TYPE: CHOOSING GAME | TONESET: s-m | TRACK: 39 |

DESCRIPTION OF GAME, ACTION OR ACTIVITY

As the children sing the song, an object representing a pie is passed round a circle. Whoever is holding the pie at the end of the song can choose a pie for the class to sing as a next verse.

As the song becomes known, invite a child to sing her choice of pie [the whole verse] while holding the pie. The class repeats this new verse as the pie is passed round the circle once more to find the next person. The class should imitate the pitch, tempo, dynamics and words of the solo child.

Singing Development: This is a very useful song for building individual confidence and careful listening to others.

Published by The Voices Foundation and Alfred Publishing Co
© The Voices Foundation 2014

I've been to Harlem

TYPE: UK CHILDREN'S GAME SONG   TONESET: l-s-m-r-d-l,-s,   TRACK: 40

DESCRIPTION OF GAME, ACTION OR ACTIVITY

Often children's songs have their origins in songs and customs from the adult world of long ago. This particular song has probable roots in a certain alcoholic drinking challenge at Harvest time in Sussex (England) when the men would take it in turns to balance a jug of beer on the top of a hat and drink the beer before the end of the second line of music, at which point they were to flip the jug into the air and catch it in the hat! Children who took the song as a basis for their own game, no doubt added the rest of the song.

Beth Hill remembers the following actions from her childhood:

At 'Harlem' and 'Dover' show respectively the deaf sign-language letters 'H' and 'D'.

At 'this wide world' make a large circle with the arm.

On the occasion of each 'over', the left hand completes a sweep across to the right hand.

For the words:

'three' – show three fingers;

'drink' – pretend to drink;

'turn the glasses' – turn the hands over;

'over' – as before.

'Sailing east' – waft hands one way; 'sailing west' – waft hands the other way.

'Sailing over the ocean' – one hand makes exaggerated wave motions.

'Better watch out' – one hand shades the eyes; 'boat begins to rock' – rock the body.

'…or you'll lose your LUNCH in the ocean' – pretend to be sea-sick, but still sing!!

Published by The Voices Foundation and Alfred Publishing Co
© The Voices Foundation 2014

Jambo jam

TYPE: SWAHILI GREETING   TONESET: s-m-d   TRACK: 41

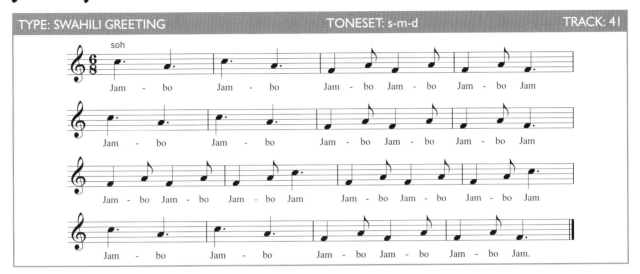

DESCRIPTION OF GAME, ACTION OR ACTIVITY

This is an east African greeting song using the Swahili word 'Jambo' meaning 'Hello'.

Facing a partner, the children's actions are as follows and correlate to the speed of the pulse:

Jambo, jambo	Wave twice with a high right hand, then twice with high left hand.
jambo, jambo, jambo, jam	In a 'high-five' position and using both hands, the partners gently touch the hands of the other, four times.
	REPEAT THE ABOVE.
Jambo, jambo, jambo, jam	Slap partner's hand right-to-right twice (two beats), then left-to-left twice (two beats) and REPEAT.
Jambo, jambo	Wave twice with a high right hand, then twice with high left hand.
jambo, jambo, jambo, jam	In a 'high-five' position and using both hands, the partners gently touch the hands of the other, four times.

John the blacksmith

TYPE: UK RHYME   TONESET: l-s-m   TRACK: 42

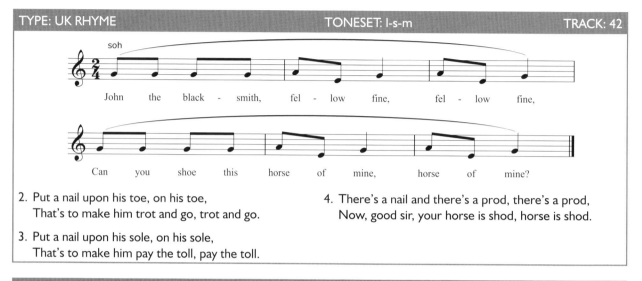

2. Put a nail upon his toe, on his toe,
   That's to make him trot and go, trot and go.

3. Put a nail upon his sole, on his sole,
   That's to make him pay the toll, pay the toll.

4. There's a nail and there's a prod, there's a prod,
   Now, good sir, your horse is shod, horse is shod.

DESCRIPTION OF GAME, ACTION OR ACTIVITY

The song might be sung as a dialogue between the horse owner and the blacksmith using two groups of singers or two solo voices.

Lots of rosy apples

TYPE: NAMING GAME   TONESET: s-m-r-d   TRACK: 43

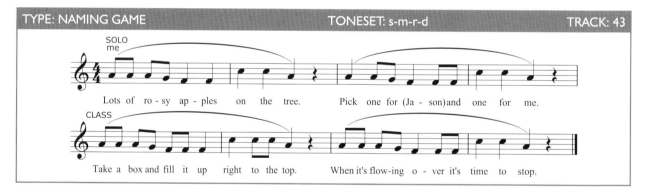

DESCRIPTION OF GAME, ACTION OR ACTIVITY

A child sings the first two phrases, naming someone in the class in the second phrase. The class sings the rest of the song, during which the first child presents a ball to the named child. Ball in hand, the named child then becomes the new leader and names a new child in the second phrase, as before.

Singing Development: It is best if all the children stand to sing this song in order to encourage the correct posture and support for the sudden leap in pitch in the middle of each phrase. It can help children who experience difficulty in raising the pitch of the voice sufficiently to stretch one arm above their heads at that moment as though 'picking a singing note higher up in the singing tree'.

Published by The Voices Foundation and Alfred Publishing Co
© The Voices Foundation 2014

Michael row the boat ashore

TYPE: USA SPIRITUAL   TONESET: l-s-f-m-r-d   TRACK: 44

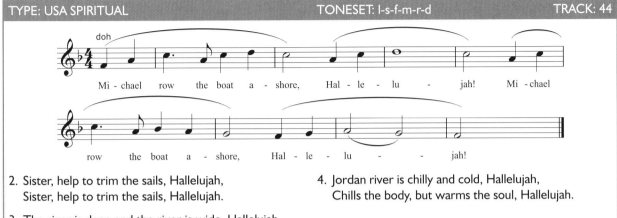

2. Sister, help to trim the sails, Hallelujah,
   Sister, help to trim the sails, Hallelujah.

3. The river is deep and the river is wide, Hallelujah,
   Milk and honey on the other side, Hallelujah.

4. Jordan river is chilly and cold, Hallelujah,
   Chills the body, but warms the soul, Hallelujah.

DESCRIPTION OF GAME, ACTION OR ACTIVITY

This spiritual was first noted down from slave singers on St Helena Island off the South Carolina coast during the American Civil War of the 1860s. The slave abolitionist, Charles Ware, had been sent to supervise the island after the plantation owners fled following the blockade by the Union navy. He heard the song and wrote it down.

YouTube: there is a video of the Cedarmont Kids singing this song with these verses.

Now the day is over

TYPE: UK HYMN   TONESET: s-f-m-r-d   TRACK: 45

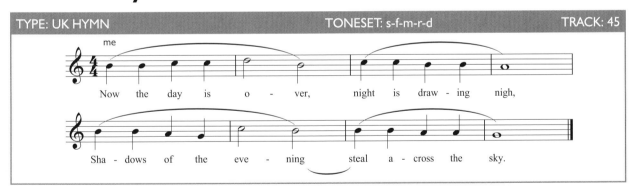

DESCRIPTION OF GAME, ACTION OR ACTIVITY

Sabine Baring Gould was a 19th century clergyman, novelist, hymn writer ['Onward Christian Soldiers'], hagiographer, landowner, eclectic scholar and father to 15 children! The words of the other seven verses of this hymn can be still found in some hymn books, although it is rarely sung these days. Children may like to write a further verse or two developing the theme of twilight and evening-time.

Singing Development: The singing should be on the quiet side without the sound becoming weak and 'breathy'. Legato [smooth] singing is essential and the tempo is slow. The sustained sound needs to be maintained through the minims [half notes] and semibreves [whole notes] allowing just sufficient time to take a relaxed breath at the commas. The second line is sung in one breath to complement the words. The whole thing requires a feeling of peace and tranquillity.

Obwisana

TYPE: GHANAIAN GAME   **TONESET: l-s-f-m-r-d**   **TRACK: 46**

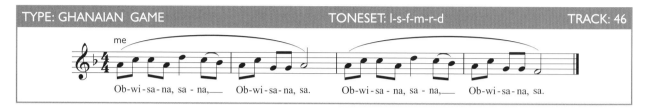

Ob-wi-sa-na, sa - na,___ Ob-wi-sa-na, sa.   Ob-wi-sa - na, sa - na,___ Ob-wi-sa-na, sa.

DESCRIPTION OF GAME, ACTION OR ACTIVITY

This is a traditional Ghanaian stick or stone-passing game. There are many variants throughout the world. The game requires team and individual concentration, co-operation and skill. It is a 'passing game' in which the kneeling circle passes objects in time with the pulse while singing the song. For indoors it is suggested that 20cm sticks cut from dowel are suitable. It is necessary to have one per person or, for certain variations of the game, two.

It is important to have a methodical and clearly directed approach to the skills of corporate stick passing in order to achieve success. It is suggested that the song and the sequence of actions are learned separately and confidence is gained before combining the two elements.

The circle of children kneels, with feet tucked under, and each person close to those on either side. It is usually better to have several circles rather than one large circle.

Game 1:

Each pupil places a stick immediately in front of the knees and pointing to the circle centre.

Assuming that the passing movement is clockwise, then each pupil places the left hand behind the back and the right hand only is used to move the stick.

To the selected tempo the circle chants *'Off we GO!'* On the word 'GO', each person takes the stick from the person <u>on their right</u> and places it in front of their knees as all sing the first syllable [*Ob-*]. The right hand returns to pick up the next stick on the second beat and places it again in front [third beat]. The rule is that no one ever picks up a stick in front of their knees.

In this way, the passing of sticks continues to a steady pulse, the song being sung twice before finishing. When errors occur, sticks may not arrive or someone in the circle finds herself with an array of unwanted sticks! When this happens, advise pupils to continue with the sequential movement to the end of the repeat, even though there may be no sticks to move!

Game 2:

As for game 1, but the sticks are passed anti-clockwise, taking a stick from the person on the left, using the left hand only.

Published by The Voices Foundation and Alfred Publishing Co
© The Voices Foundation 2014

Old King Glory

TYPE: USA STREET GAME   TONESET: s-f-m-r-d-l,-s,   TRACK: 47

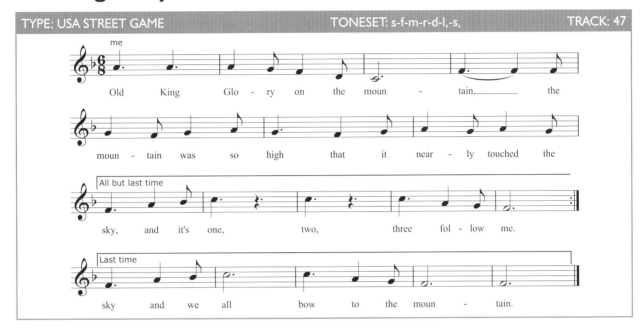

Old King Glo - ry on the moun - tain, _____ the

moun - tain was so high that it near - ly touched the

All but last time

sky, and it's one, two, three fol - low me.

Last time

sky and we all bow to the moun - tain.

DESCRIPTION OF GAME, ACTION OR ACTIVITY

The children form a circle with joined hands and a leader standing outside the circle.

All circle clockwise, as the leader walks round the outside in the opposite direction.

At the words *one, two, three*, the leader taps three adjacent pupils on the shoulder. These children leave the circle, the first placing a hand on the leader's shoulder with the second and third following in the same way, thus creating a four-person line.

The circle gap is closed and the song and actions are repeated several times until a long line led by the leader is circling a short circle.

Eventually the old circle disintegrates and the long line joins to form the new circle.

Published by The Voices Foundation and Alfred Publishing Co
© The Voices Foundation 2014

Oliver Twist

TYPE: UK STREET GAME   TONESET: l-s-m   TRACK: 48

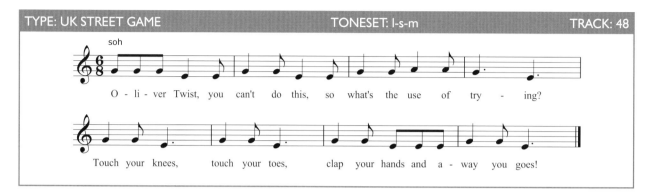

DESCRIPTION OF GAME, ACTION OR ACTIVITY

Children stand facing a partner in two concentric circles (inner and outer).

Actions for:

'Oliver Twist, you can't do this, so what's the use of trying'

   Clap own hands, right hand with partner, clap own hands, left hand with partner. Do this 2x

'Touch your knees'

   Tap knees 2x

'Touch your toes'

   Tap toes 2x

'Clap your hands'

   Two claps

'Away you goes'

   Everyone in the outside circle moves clockwise and the song starts again with a new partner

One for the mouse

TYPE: UK RHYME   TONESET: m-r-d   TRACK: 49

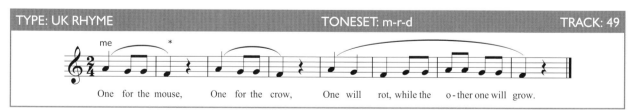

DESCRIPTION OF GAME, ACTION OR ACTIVITY

This very simple melody invites several interesting possibilities for singing in two-part canon.

Using the melody as written the second voice enters two beats after the first.

Invert the pitch of the melody, ie start on F doh [d r r m / F G G A etc.] and the second voice enters two beats after the first. Initially sing to singing names [sol-fa].

Published by The Voices Foundation and Alfred Publishing Co
© The Voices Foundation 2014

Oo-a-lay-lay

TYPE: POLYNESIAN ECHO GAME   TONESET: l-s-m-r-d   TRACK: 50

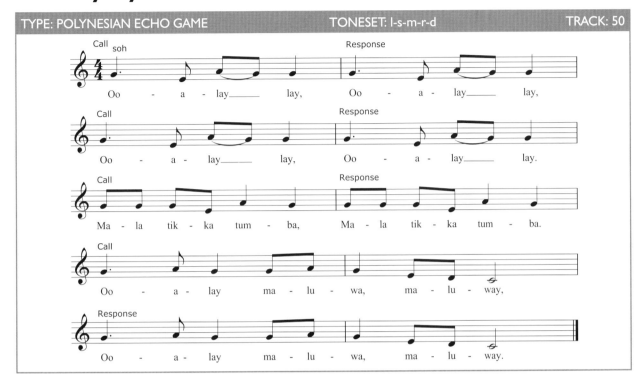

DESCRIPTION OF GAME, ACTION OR ACTIVITY

The leader sings the first 'call' and performs an action of their choice, one that the class can copy. They must also match the pitch, tempo and dynamics of the leader. The leader must be able to keep a steady tempo throughout and not falter because of the physical actions.

The leader may:

- keep the same action throughout

- change the action when the song is repeated

- change the action for every 'call'

- repeat a previous action when he/she wishes

Pease pudding hot

TYPE: TRADITIONAL RHYME   TONESET: f-m-r-d   TRACK: 51

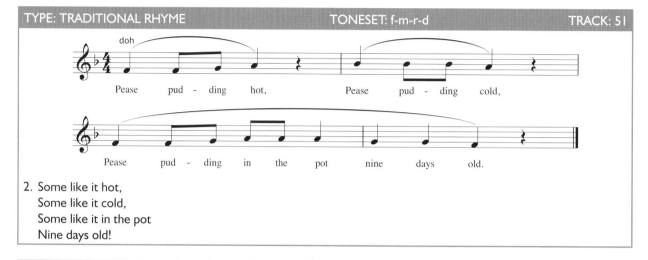

2. Some like it hot,
   Some like it cold,
   Some like it in the pot
   Nine days old!

DESCRIPTION OF GAME, ACTION OR ACTIVITY

The class form circle-groups of six to eight. Each child contributes one hand in a 'hand-pile' to represent the pease pudding. While singing the song to a steady tempo, as each pulse is felt the hand at the bottom of the pile is pulled out and placed on the top. All movements should be made accurately with the pulse.

For adventurous pupils!
Working in pairs, the children are asked to devise a handclapping sequence, performing to the feel of the pulse. The sequence should be their own invention and might be performed for others to watch.

Published by The Voices Foundation and Alfred Publishing Co
© The Voices Foundation 2014

Peel bananas

TYPE: ACTION SONG   TONESET: d-l-s   TRACK: 52

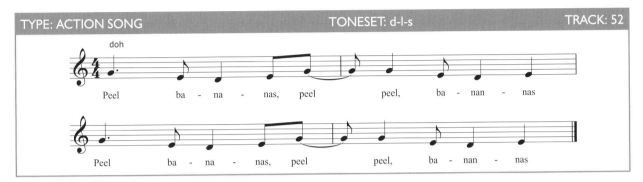

DESCRIPTION OF GAME, ACTION OR ACTIVITY

Children stand in a circle with hands by sides. They allow plenty of space between each other and do the following actions for each verse.

1. 'Form banana..........'

   Right hand slowly raises to be above the head. Left hand follows on the 2nd phrase [8 beats each]

2. 'Peel banana............'

   Right hand comes back down, making a twisting movement at the wrist; left hand follows

3. 'Chop banana..........'

   Left hand is held flat and right hand chops on top 8 times; reverse for other hand

4. 'Mash banana..........'

   Right hand forms a fist and 'mashes' into left hand; reverse for other hand

5. 'Blend banana..........'

   Imagining holding a big blender the right hand makes a circular movement; left hand does the same

6. 'Pour banana............'

   Left hand forms a cup shape and right hand 'pours' into it from a height; reverse for other hand

7. 'Drink banana..........'

   Right hand forms cup shape and everyone pretends to drink; then with left hand

8. 'Yum banana..........'

   Right hand rubs tummy in a circular motion; swap and do with left hand

Feel free to invent with the children other actions, for example, 'Go bananas!'

Plainie clappie

TYPE: UK BALL GAME   TONESET: l-s-m   TRACK: 53

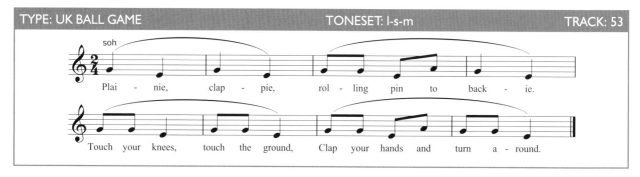

DESCRIPTION OF GAME, ACTION OR ACTIVITY

Originally this was a ball game in which a child threw a tennis ball against the wall, allowing it to bounce on the ground in front before catching it. This was repeated over and over again as the child chanted the rhyme. The words suggest actions that have to be carried out by the child as she continues to bounce the ball against the wall. Children might be given the opportunity to play this outside.

Actions:

Plainie = no action
clappie = clap hands twice
rolling pin to = rolling hands round each other
backie = clap behind back
The other words are self-explanatory.

For an indoor version a circle is formed with a child in the centre. The ball is bounced on the floor to a person in the circle to catch and who must then return it in the same way. The centre pupil then bounces the ball to the next person in the circle who returns the ball in the same way – and so on. The action of 'bounce-catch' is done to a two-beat pattern. As this takes place, everyone in the circle including the catcher chants and performs the actions suggested by the words. Failure of the 'catcher' to do the action, or dropping the ball means the child must sit down until another person fails, at which point he/she can recommence participation in the game, while the other person sits.

Published by The Voices Foundation and Alfred Publishing Co
© The Voices Foundation 2014

Rain is falling down

TYPE: WEATHER SONG   TONESET: m-r-d   TRACK: 54

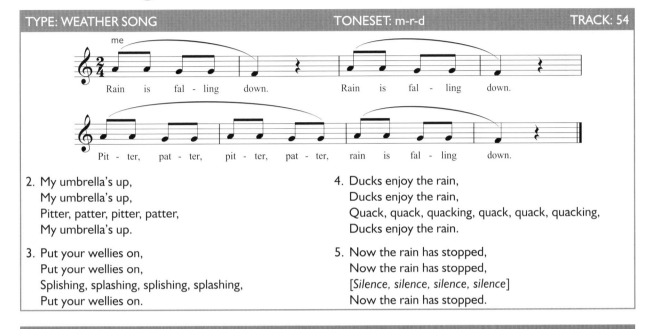

2. My umbrella's up,
   My umbrella's up,
   Pitter, patter, pitter, patter,
   My umbrella's up.

3. Put your wellies on,
   Put your wellies on,
   Splishing, splashing, splishing, splashing,
   Put your wellies on.

4. Ducks enjoy the rain,
   Ducks enjoy the rain,
   Quack, quack, quacking, quack, quack, quacking,
   Ducks enjoy the rain.

5. Now the rain has stopped,
   Now the rain has stopped,
   [Silence, silence, silence, silence]
   Now the rain has stopped.

DESCRIPTION OF GAME, ACTION OR ACTIVITY

In verse 5, phrase 3, the singers use their Thinking Voices.

The children might be creative in writing another verse or two on the subject of rain or any other kind of weather.

Rain on the green grass

TYPE: UK RHYME   TONESET: s-d   TRACK: 55

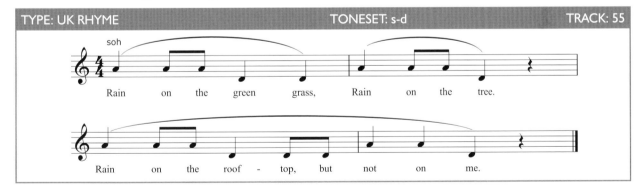

DESCRIPTION OF GAME, ACTION OR ACTIVITY

There are just two levels of pitch used in this rhyme, a higher sound and a lower sound. The children hold their unpreferred-hand, palm facing the body and fingers slightly spread. The index finger of the other hand is used as a 'pointer'. Using the thumb for the higher sound and the smallest finger for the lowest sound, the 'pointer' moves between the two. The song starts on the higher sound. Can the children move appropriately from pitch to pitch as the song is sung?

Published by The Voices Foundation and Alfred Publishing Co
© The Voices Foundation 2014

Rain, rain, go away

TYPE: UK TRADITIONAL RHYME   TONESET: l-s-m   TRACK: 56

Rain, rain, go a - way, Come a - gain an - oth - er day.

2. Which day shall I come?
   Come again on Monday
   (Tuesday, Wednesday...)

3. Sunshine's here to stay,
   Now we can go out to play.

DESCRIPTION OF GAME, ACTION OR ACTIVITY

The class chooses a day of the week and, after singing verse 1, a child representing a 'rain cloud' sings phrase 1 of verse 2: "Which day shall I come?" The class replies, using the words, "Come again on Monday, Tuesday, etc.", until the agreed day of the week is reached. The last verse is used to bring the song to a close.

Rise, sun, awaken

TYPE: PAWNEE NATION USA   TONESET: l-r-d-l,-s,   TRACK: 57

Rise, sun, a - wa - ken, Send your warmth to earth be - low, Send your light for this new day, Rise, sun, a - wa - ken. Rise, sun, rise.

DESCRIPTION OF GAME, ACTION OR ACTIVITY

The Pawnee nation was one of the great tribes of older America. They lived and largely farmed in various regions during their days of freedom, but more latterly in the Great Plains of what is now the state of Nebraska. Their religious rituals involved worship of the Sun and Moon and a belief that these gave birth to the first man, and the Morning and Evening Stars produced the first woman. The Pawnee people now number about 3,500.

Published by The Voices Foundation and Alfred Publishing Co
© The Voices Foundation 2014

Rocky mountain

TYPE: USA TRADITION   TONESET: l-s-m-r-d   TRACK: 58

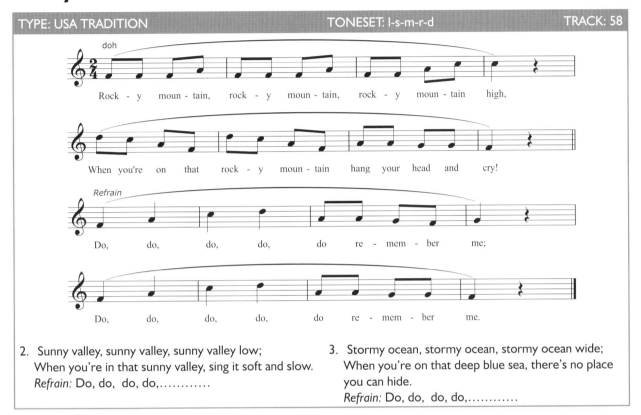

Rock - y moun - tain, rock - y moun - tain, rock - y moun - tain high,

When you're on that rock - y moun - tain hang your head and cry!

Refrain

Do, do, do, do, do re - mem - ber me;

Do, do, do, do, do re - mem - ber me.

2. Sunny valley, sunny valley, sunny valley low;
   When you're in that sunny valley, sing it soft and slow.
   Refrain: Do, do, do, do,............

3. Stormy ocean, stormy ocean, stormy ocean wide;
   When you're on that deep blue sea, there's no place
   you can hide.
   Refrain: Do, do, do, do,............

DESCRIPTION OF GAME, ACTION OR ACTIVITY

Singing Development: This is a useful song for encouraging children to think and to use techniques that help to ensure in-tune singing.

With rising pitch, singers have to increase the diaphragm muscle support. The danger is that the singer will fractionally undershoot the correct pitch (sing 'flat'), especially between soh and lah. They could *think* of the image of a basketball having to enter the basket from above and not onto the rim of the basket. However, the breath support effort requires *downward thinking* ie anchoring the muscle effort around the waist and lower!

Descending pitch over a series of notes, especially when recurring in this way and with a large upward interval leap in between, can lead to *slack diaphragm muscle support*, a failure to fully negotiate the leaps and inadequate support for the descending pitches. To compensate with descending pitch phrases, the singer should *think upwards*.

Row, boat, row

TYPE: UK RHYME   TONESET: l-s-m   TRACK: 59

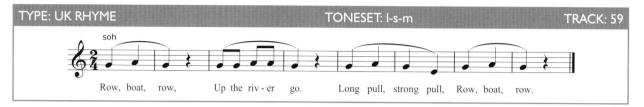

Row, boat, row, Up the riv-er go. Long pull, strong pull, Row, boat, row.

DESCRIPTION OF GAME, ACTION OR ACTIVITY

The song can be used as a sort of shanty song in which each pupil pulls on an 'oar' in time to the pulse.

The children should start with arms out in front and pull in on the first beat, as the first word is sung. The oar-arms are moved out on the second beat - and so on.

A leader sets the tempo by tapping four steady beats before the singing starts.

Salani

TYPE: MALAWI FAREWELL SONG   TONESET: l-s-m-r-d   TRACK: 60

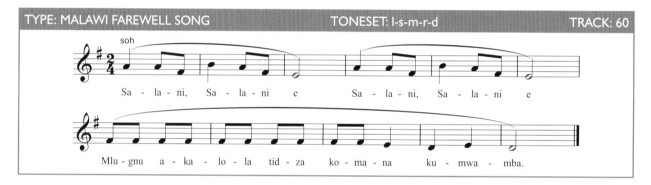

Sa - la - ni, Sa - la - ni e   Sa - la - ni, Sa - la - ni e

Mlu - gnu a - ka - lo - la tid - za ko - ma - na ku - mwa - mba.

DESCRIPTION OF GAME, ACTION OR ACTIVITY

Malawians have long been travellers and migrants and so farewells often take place. This song is typical. The meaning of the lyrics is:

"Farewell now, may you fare well. Please God, we may all meet together again, meet above."

Pronunciation: Chewa [or Chichewa] is the national indigenous language of Malawi and, like similar African languages, is not difficult to pronounce. All the letters sound and they run very easily with the vowels. Pronounce 'a' as 'ar'[bravo]; 'i' as 'ee'.

See other greeting and farewell songs in this programme in French, English, Swahili and Shona.

Published by The Voices Foundation and Alfred Publishing Co
© The Voices Foundation 2014

Salut! Ça va?

| TYPE: FRENCH GREETING | TONESET: : s-m-r-d | TRACK: 61 |

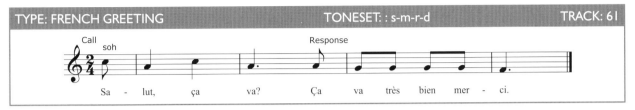

DESCRIPTION OF GAME, ACTION OR ACTIVITY

This is a French greeting with a response.

The greeting in English translation is, *"Hello, how are you?"* and the response is, *"I'm very well, thank you."*

The response could be: "Ça va très bien, et toi?" [...and you?]

Say, boom, chicka boom

| TYPE: CAMP FIRE | TONESET: Chant | TRACK: 62 |

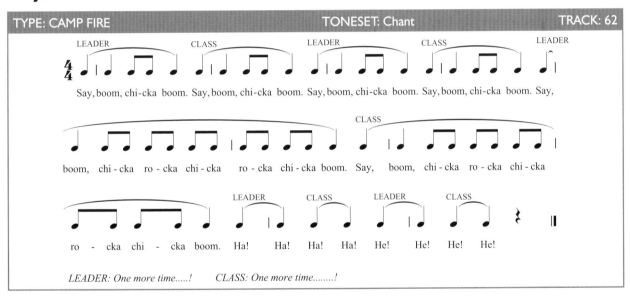

DESCRIPTION OF GAME, ACTION OR ACTIVITY

This 'copy-me' chant has a long-standing tradition at campfire social situations, particularly scouts.

The leader has to be imaginative and challenging, while still retaining control of the tempo and only making realistic and safe demands on others.

Each repeat by the same leader can feature a change of tempo and dynamics, voice inflections including singing, whispering, pitch and distortion.

Published by The Voices Foundation and Alfred Publishing Co
© The Voices Foundation 2014

Sorida

TYPE: ZIMBABWE GREETING   TONESET: s-m-d   TRACK: 63

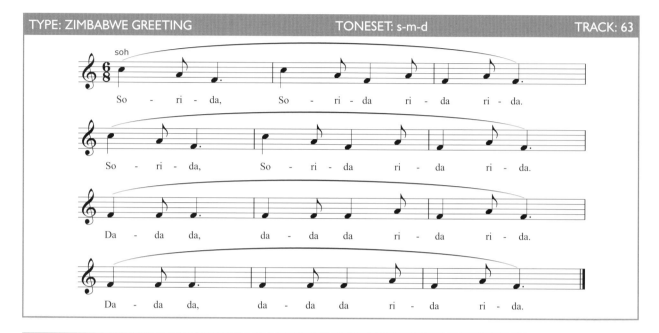

So - ri - da,   So - ri - da ri - da ri - da.

So - ri - da,   So - ri - da ri - da ri - da.

Da - da da,   da - da da ri - da ri - da.

Da - da da,   da - da da ri - da ri - da.

DESCRIPTION OF GAME, ACTION OR ACTIVITY

This is a Shona language greeting song akin to 'Jambo' (Swahili) and 'Shalom' (Hebrew).

Singing Development: In an attempt to suggest two people approaching each other from a distance to greet each other, the song starts quietly and grows louder as it progresses. In this case, Group A or Child A sings phrase 1, Group B or Child B answers with phrase 2; A sings phrase 3 and B sings phrase 4. The children need to listen carefully and respond appropriately in order to achieve an even and incremental dynamic, one that does not result in 'shout-singing'. Engage the pupils in assessing how well the performance achieved its goal. Select two children to act as assessors by listening rather than singing.

Compare the Malawian farewell song, 'Salani'.

Published by The Voices Foundation and Alfred Publishing Co
© The Voices Foundation 2014

Spinning top

TYPE: SONG   TONESET: s-m-d   TRACK: 64

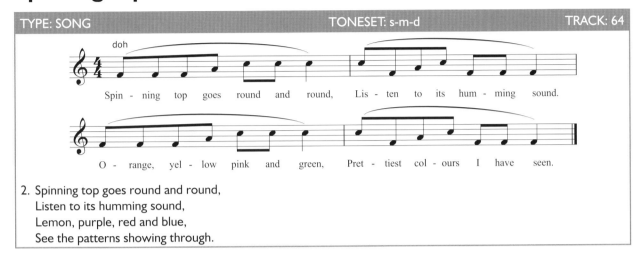

Spin - ning top goes round and round, Lis - ten to its hum - ming sound.

O - range, yel - low pink and green, Pret - tiest col - ours I have seen.

2. Spinning top goes round and round,
   Listen to its humming sound,
   Lemon, purple, red and blue,
   See the patterns showing through.

DESCRIPTION OF GAME, ACTION OR ACTIVITY

When the song has been well learned, the following activities are possible:

The class sings the song and then immediately hums the melody.

The class is divided into two groups. Group A sings the song, then Group B hums the song. The two groups then sing and hum simultaneously.

A humming/spinning top is set in motion and the song is sung to accompany it.

Practise humming the pitch of 'doh' with Group A, each note lasting for four beats. Practise humming the note 'soh' with Group B, each note lasting for four beats. Both of these 'drones' are then sung simultaneously to represent the sound of the spinning top. Start with two four-beats-worth of 'drones' before singing the song. This is a good introduction to singing in parts. When the children are confident, divide the class into three groups, two to continuously sing the drones and after two four-beat hums, the third group to sing the song. The drone groups take a short breath towards the end of each four beats. When there has been success with three groups, invite three children to perform the song in the same way.

Published by The Voices Foundation and Alfred Publishing Co
© The Voices Foundation 2014

Starlight, star bright

TYPE: WISHING RHYME   TONESET: l-s-m-r-d   TRACK: 65

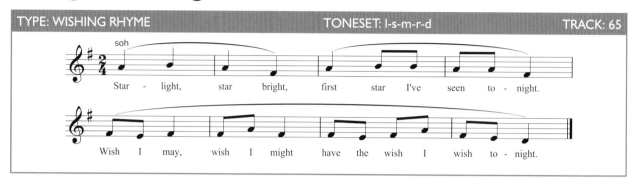

Star - light, star bright, first star I've seen to - night.

Wish I may, wish I might have the wish I wish to - night.

DESCRIPTION OF GAME, ACTION OR ACTIVITY

The words are those of a traditional wishing rhyme, probably said by children in the past as they got into bed for the night.

The children kneel in a circle, with one child holding a comfortably large ball. During the singing of the song the ball is passed in time to the pulse, and whoever holds the ball on the last sound is encouraged to make a secret wish. A 'wisher' may choose to share his wish with everyone.

Published by The Voices Foundation and Alfred Publishing Co
© The Voices Foundation 2014

Summer goodbye

TYPE: GERMAN FOLKSONG   TONESET: s-f-m-r-d   TRACK: 66

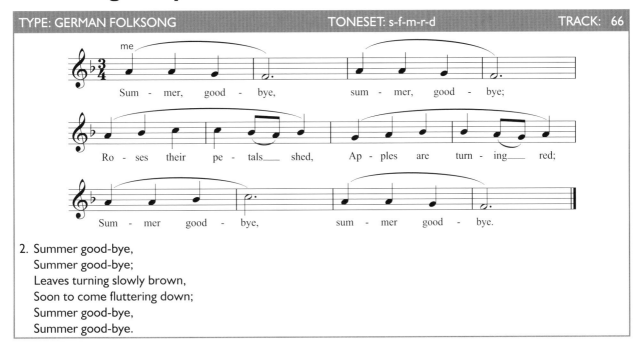

2. Summer good-bye,
   Summer good-bye;
   Leaves turning slowly brown,
   Soon to come fluttering down;
   Summer good-bye,
   Summer good-bye.

DESCRIPTION OF GAME, ACTION OR ACTIVITY

The German text is:

Winter ade! Scheiden tut weh.
Aber dein Scheiden macht,
Dass mir das Herze lacht.
Winter ade! Scheiden tut weh.
["Winter goodbye!"]

Singing Development: The singing should be warm with a wide open-throat approach to the sound of the vowels and also very *legato* in style. Aim for two phrases to one breath. The tuning needs care: phrases such as three and four, with rising and falling pitch, can cause problems. Ask the pupils to 'think-upwards', keeping together the diaphragm muscle strength during these phrases. Also the rising pitch of the penultimate phrase needs extra concentration and focus.

Divide the class into two groups. Group A performs the first phrase, Group B the second phrase, Group A the third phrase and so on. Ask a 'pupil-conductor' to conduct the song, showing with left and right hands when she feels a group should sing the next new phrase. This would be without preliminary discussion and would require the conductor to feel and identify the phrase lengths. After several performances, a discussion might take place about the relative merits of each conductor's phrase-length decisions.

Suo gân

TYPE: WELSH LULLABY   TONESET: m-r-d   TRACK: 67

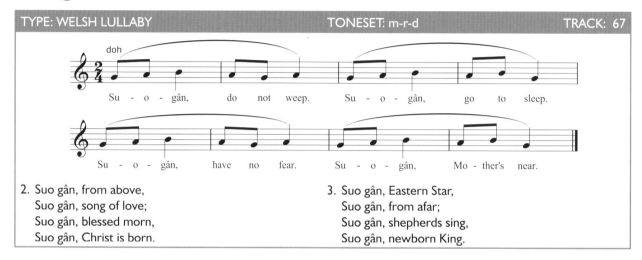

2. Suo gân, from above,
   Suo gân, song of love;
   Suo gân, blessed morn,
   Suo gân, Christ is born.

3. Suo gân, Eastern Star,
   Suo gân, from afar;
   Suo gân, shepherds sing,
   Suo gân, newborn King.

DESCRIPTION OF GAME, ACTION OR ACTIVITY

The song's title simply means lullaby (*suo* = lull; *gân* = song).

The additional verses might make this song a useful Nativity song or Christmas concert item.

Singing Development: Ask the children to sing gently and with a smooth, swaying feel. They should try to make each singing sound connect to another like beads close together on a necklace: this is *legato* singing.

Tony Chestnut

TYPE: ACTION SONG   TONESET: l-s-f-m-r-d   TRACK: 68

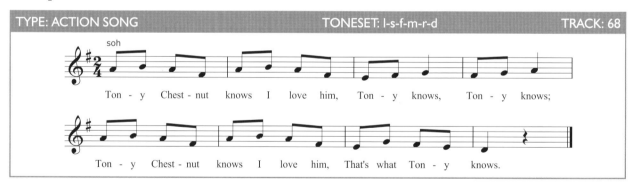

DESCRIPTION OF GAME, ACTION OR ACTIVITY

Sing the song with the actions as described below:

To -	touch toe
- ny	touch knee
Chest -	touch chest
- nut	touch head
knows	touch nose
I	touch eye
love him	touch heart x 2

Published by The Voices Foundation and Alfred Publishing Co
© The Voices Foundation 2014

We can sing high

TYPE: TEACHING SONG	TONESET: s'-m-r-d -s,	TRACK: 69

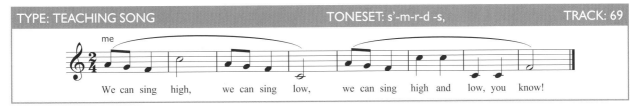

DESCRIPTION OF GAME, ACTION OR ACTIVITY

This is a useful song for the early stages of teaching pitch and in introducing the minim [half note] rhythm value.

It can also be adapted for giving early two-part singing experience:

Two groups; group A sings phrase 1 and sustains the last note on 'high' while group B sings phrase 2

Group B in turn sustains the last note of phrase 2 ['low'] while group A sings phrase 3

Both groups sing the last two notes, 'you know!'

With some two-part singing experience behind them, the class can sing the melody as a canon, ie group A starts and on reaching the word 'high', group B starts from the beginning and follows group A who have continued with the song.

Published by The Voices Foundation and Alfred Publishing Co

Listening Material

Published by The Voices Foundation and Alfred Publishing Co
© The Voices Foundation 2014

Listening Material

BADINERIE	UNIT 1	TRACK 70
Composer	Johann Sebastian Bach	
Performer	Capella Istropolitana / Jaroslav Dvorák	
Time	1'30"	
Source	Naxos	

Bach [1685–1750] was appointed chief musician to the Court orchestra at Anhalt-Cöthen in 1717. Much of his music for instruments alone was written there, including this piece for solo flute and string orchestra, part of a collection of short movements known as *Suite No. 2*. The word *Badinerie* is derived from the French meaning 'jesting'.

LE COUCOU	UNIT 2	TRACK 71
Composer	Louis-Claude Daquin	
Performer	Martin Souter	
Time	2'13"	
Source	The Gift of Music label	

Daquin was a much respected keyboard player and organist in France during the 18th century. This lively cameo of the cuckoo's call was part of a suite of short pieces written in 1735.

PARADE	UNIT 3	TRACK 72
Composer	Jacques Ibert	
Performer	Orchestre des Concerts Lamoureux/Sado	
Time	2'00"	
Source	Naxos	

'Parade' is one of a group of pieces that Ibert selected from his music for the play, 'The Italian Straw Hat', and collectively called them 'Divertissement' [1930]. The listener is placed in one spot and witnesses a parade with marching band, approach, pass by and recede down the road.

CLOG DANCE	UNIT 5	TRACK 73
Composer	Peter Hertel/Lanchbery	
Performer	Royal Opera House Orchestra/Lanchbery	
Time	2'17"	
Source	Decca	

This music was incorporated into the ever-popular Frederick Ashton 1960 choreography of the ballet 'La fille mal gardée' ['The wayward daughter']. Lise, the daughter of the Widow Simone, tempts her mother with a pair of wooden clogs. Simone performs a hilarious dance in them, attempting, among things, to 'stand on points'.

YouTube: there is currently a video of The Royal Ballet performing this dance.

Published by The Voices Foundation and Alfred Publishing Co
© The Voices Foundation 2014

THE BIRD, THE DUCK, THE CAT	UNIT 5	TRACKS 74, 75, 76
Composer	Sergei Prokofiev	
Performer	Slovak Radio Symphony Orchestra/Lenard	
Time	4'52"	
Source	Naxos	

In 1936 Prokofiev wrote the story, text and music for *Peter and the Wolf*. The plot concerns Peter at his grandfather's house where there are several animals all living in fear of a wolf. The latter comes one day and all take flight, Peter into a tree. By clever ploy Peter manages to lasso the wolf. Huntsmen appear and take the wolf away. In the narrated story, each character is represented by an instrument and its own melody, eg the bird by the flute; the duck by the oboe; the cat by the clarinet.

THE SWAN	UNIT 6, 10	TRACK 77
Composer	Camille Saint-Saëns	
Performer	Slovak Radio Symphony Orchestra/Lenard	
Time	3'07"	
Source	Naxos	

Saint-Saëns wrote his *Carnival of the Animals* in 1886 as a 'piece of fun', a collection of animal portraits. This piece for solo cello accompanied by two pianos depicts the grace of the swan gliding across the water. One piano provides a water ripple effect while the other suggests the movement of the feet.

THE VIENNESE MUSICAL CLOCK	UNIT 7	TRACK 78
Composer	Zoltán Kodály	
Performer	London Philharmonic Orchestra/Solti	
Time	2'06"	
Source	Naxos	

Kodály is much respected composer and philosopher of music education. His opera, 'Háry János', concerns an old man recalling to tavern listeners exaggerated accounts of his exploits as a brave young soldier. One such tale is how Háry rescued the Emperor of Austria's daughter from the Russians and brought her back to Vienna where everything was strange and fantastic. The most marvellous thing that he saw there was a huge clock. When it chimed the hour, doors opened and a procession of clockwork soldiers emerged to marching music.

Published by The Voices Foundation and Alfred Publishing Co
© The Voices Foundation 2014

MARCH	UNIT 7	TRACK 79
Composer	Pyotr Tchaikovsky	
Performer	Slovak Radio Symphony Orchestra/Lenard	
Time	2'30"	
Source	Naxos	

This piece is one of the movements that Tchaikovsky wrote for the ballet, *The Nutcracker*, in 1892. The ballet is based on E.T.A. Hoffmann's story *The Nutcracker and the Mouse King*. It is Christmas Eve and excited children play around the tree before presents are given out.

WHERE ARE YOU?	UNIT 7	TRACK 80
Composer	Traditional	
Performer	Balalaika Ensemble Wolga	
Time	1'11"	
Source	ARC Music	

The balalaika is a three-stringed instrument of Russian origin. The body of the instrument is triangular in shape with a fretted fingerboard and played in the manner of the guitar. The instrument is built in various sizes, which enable a wide range of pitch to be used and for the players to play as groups or even orchestras.

IN THE HALL OF THE MOUNTAIN KING	UNIT 8	TRACK 81
Composer	Edvard Grieg	
Performer	Malmo Symphony Orchestra/Engeset	
Time	2'40"	
Source	Naxos	

The piece forms part of the incidental music written for the Ibsen play, 'Peer Gynt', in 1876. In a dream-like fantasy, Peer Gynt enters the great hall of the Mountain King: "There is a great crowd of troll courtiers, gnomes and goblins. The Old Man sits on his throne, with crown and sceptre, surrounded by his children and relatives. Peer Gynt stands before him. There is a tremendous uproar in the hall."

PERCUSSION	UNIT 9	TRACK 82
Composer	Benjamin Britten	
Performer	London Symphony Orchestra/Bedford	
Time	1'55"	
Source	Naxos	

In 1946 Britten was commissioned to write music for an educational documentary film, *Instruments of the Orchestra*, now more generally known as *The Young Person's Guide to the Orchestra*. Britten took a melody by the 17th century composer, Henry Purcell to start the work, and then devised a series of variations on it for each section of the symphony orchestra, giving each instrument a solo role as well. He combines the whole orchestra once again in a brilliant Finale.

Published by The Voices Foundation and Alfred Publishing Co

O EUCHARI	UNIT 10	TRACK 83
Composer	Hildegard of Bingen	
Performer	Oxford Camerata/Summerly	
Time	2'22"	
Source	Naxos Educational	

Saint Hildegard of Bingen was a 12th century Benedictine abbess, composer, visionary and polymath. Over 70 of her compositions survive, including music for a Mystery Play. Her melody is noted for its beauty, soaring upward phrases and originality for the time.

NUN, GIMEL, HEI, SHIN	UNIT 11	TRACK 84
Composer	Judith Shatin	
Performer	New London Children's Choir/Cope	
Time	2'15"	
Source	Naxos	

Among the customs of the Jewish festival of Hanukka are the games for children, being in part instructive and part sheer good fun. On the dreidl, a spinning top, are the initial letters of 'nes gadol haya sham' [a great miracle happened here], in phonetic Hebrew, 'nun, gimel, hei, shin'. The phrase refers to the miracle of the oil lamp within the restored Temple of Jerusalem many centuries ago. This piece reflects the gathering momentum of the dreidl with voices singing in round and a solo voice referring to the flat cakes cooked in oil at the time of the festival.

OLIVER CROMWELL	UNIT 11	TRACK 85
Composer	Benjamin Britten	
Performer	Philip Langridge/Johnson	
Time	0'45"	
Source	Naxos	

This rhyme has its origins in 17th century Suffolk. It is a piece of blatant satire at Cromwell's expense and, like other so-called nursery rhymes, started life as a piece of adult political humour.

THE ARRIVAL OF THE QUEEN OF SHEBA	UNIT 11	TRACK 86
Composer	George Handel	
Performer	Frankfurt Baroque Orchestra/Martini	
Time	3'06"	
Source	Naxos	

In 1749 Handel completed a major composition based on the Biblical account of the visit by the Queen of Sheba to the Israelite court of King Solomon. This piece has often been used by brides for their own entrance music at the start of the marriage ceremony.

Published by The Voices Foundation and Alfred Publishing Co
© The Voices Foundation 2014

TOCCATA	UNIT 12	TRACK 87
Composer	Thomas Pitfield	
Performer	Peter Donohoe	
Time	1'57"	
Source	Naxos	

Thomas Pitfield [1903–1999] was a skilled composer, poet, engraver, artist, furniture maker, calligrapher and teacher who lived all his life in northwest England. He wrote music for many famous performers and for widely varied groups of instruments and singers.

O POLICHINELO	REVISION UNIT A	TRACK 88
Composer	Heitor Villa-Lobos	
Performer	Sonia Rubinsky	
Time	1'52"	
Source	Naxos	

This is one of a group of pieces written under the title, 'Prole do Bebê' [Baby's Toys], by probably the most significant figure in 20th century Brazilian art music. Here we have a lively portrayal of the impish behaviour of someone British children know as Mr Punch.

YouTube: there are a number of videos, some with two pianists, some by a soloist, fascinating for children to watch the fast movement of the fingers.

A POBREZINHA	REVISION UNIT A	TRACK 89
Composer	Heitor Villa-Lobos	
Performer	Sonia Rubinsky	
Time	2'21"	
Source	Naxos	

Another piece from 'Prole do Bebê' in which the rag doll is pictured as a floppy, well-worn but much loved toy.

BYDŁO	UNIT 13	TRACK 90
Composer	Modest Mussorgsky	
Performer	Ukraine National Orchestra/Kuchar	
Time	3'17"	
Source	Naxos	

The composer asks the listener to walk through a picture gallery and stop to contemplate certain paintings that take his fancy. The picture of a 'Bydło' is one of a heavy, lumbering ox cart. The suggestion is that the cart is passing the observer and eventually recedes into the distance. 'Bydło' is one of a series of 'pictures' that Mussorgsky wrote as 'Pictures at an Exhibition' in 1874.

YouTube: there are currently videos of an orchestra playing this piece, great for children to watch and follow the tuba player.

Published by The Voices Foundation and Alfred Publishing Co
© The Voices Foundation 2014

FLIGHT OF THE BUMBLEBEE	UNIT 13	TRACK 91
Composer	Nikolay Rimsky-Korsakov	
Performer	CSR Symphony Orchestra/Bramhall	
Time	1'34"	
Source	Naxos	

This piece closes Act III of the opera, 'The Tale of Tsar Saltan' [1900], during which the magic Song Bird changes the Tsar's son into an insect so that he can fly away to visit his father.

YouTube: there are several videos of arrangements for solo instruments. Among the stunning performances look out for the pianist, Yuja Wang.

THE GREEN MAN	UNIT 13	TRACK 92
Composer	Anonymous	
Performer	Estampie/Derrick	
Time	0'55"	
Source	Naxos Early	

The title of this ancient dance tune is derived from the sculptures, drawings and other representations of a face with leaves and greenery sprouting from various orifices on the head. The character probably has pagan roots, but can be seen in decorative medieval church embellishments of stone and wood. The melody first appeared in 'Playford's Dancing Master' collection of 1651.

SANGVA DUVA	UNIT 14	TRACK 93
Composer	Tibetan Buddhist Chant	
Performer	Dip Tse Chok Ling Monastery Monks	
Time	1'29"	
Source	Naxos Educational	

This Tibetan chant is an integral part of Buddhist worship and ceremony. The text is often complex, but basically the music is Yang chanting over very low open throat syllables.

ARABIAN DANCE	UNIT 15	TRACK 94
Composer	Pyotr Tchaikovsky	
Performer	Slovak Philharmonic Orchestra/Halász	
Time	2'55"	
Source	Naxos	

In *The Nutcracker* ballet story, the Prince escorts Clara to the Land of Sweets where the Sugar Plum Fairy greets them. The Prince tells her about their daring battle with the army of mice and she rewards them with a celebration that includes this dance.

THE TYPEWRITER	UNIT 16	TRACK 95
Composer	Leroy Anderson	
Performer	BBC Concert Orchestra/Slatkin	
Time	1'43"	
Source	Naxos	

The composer wrote many light-music classics during the mid-1900s, including 'Sleigh Ride', 'Syncopated Clock', 'Bugler's Holiday' and 'Blue Tango', all with instant appeal, but his clever writing gave them timeless appeal, too.

YouTube: among the various uploads is one featuring the percussionist, Martin Breinschmid, performing on an actual typewriter – great fun to see and hear!

UNDER THE GREENWOOD TREE	UNIT 17	TRACK 96
Composer	Anonymous	
Performer	Estampie/Derrick	
Time	0'34"	
Source	Naxos Early	

This is a simple English dance tune whose title has resonances of Shakespeare's play, As You Like It, Act Two, when Amiens sings a song starting with these words. Thomas Hardy wrote a novel Under the Greenwood Tree in which there is a country-dance party.

O PASTOR ANIMARUM	UNIT 17	TRACK 97
Composer	Hildegard of Bingen	
Performer	Oxford Camerata/Summerly	
Time	1'29"	
Source	Naxos Early	

Latin was the language of the church in the middle ages. This chant asks for 'the shepherd of souls' to liberate us from our 'miseries and languishing'. Saint Hildegard of Bingen was a 12th century Benedictine abbess, composer, visionary and polymath.

PAVANE	UNIT 18	TRACK 98
Composer	Peter Warlock	
Performer	Bournemouth Sinfonietta/Studt	
Time	1'56"	
Source	Naxos	

The pavane was a stately dance for the 16th century aristocracy, having its origins in Italy. The pavane's basic movement consisted of forward and backward steps; the couples rose onto the balls of their feet and swayed from side to side. Warlock's piece is a 20th century pastiche.

Published by The Voices Foundation and Alfred Publishing Co
© The Voices Foundation 2014

TEMPO'S BOOGIE	UNIT 19	TRACK 99
Composer	Lionel Hampton	
Performer	Lionel Hampton and Orchestra	
Time	3'04"	
Source	Naxos Jazz Legends	

Boogie-woogie is an African American style of piano-based blues that became popular in the late 1930s, but originated much earlier. While the blues traditionally depicts a range of emotions, boogie-woogie is associated with dancing. The music is largely characterised by the repetitive 'jumpy' bass motif.

OSTINATO	UNIT 20	TRACK 100
Composer	Gustav Holst	
Performer	Bournemouth Sinfonietta/Studt	
Time	1'57"	
Source	Naxos	

Ostinato is a word derived from Italian meaning 'obstinate' or 'stubborn'. In music it refers to a repetitive feature, rhythmic only or melodic, that is largely unchanging. This musical device has a very long history in music. Ravel's 'Bolero' is a well-known example. The more recent 'riff' is very similar with examples such as, The Kinks in 'You really got me' and Radiohead in 'Creep'.

CHINESE DANCE	UNIT 21	TRACK 101
Composer	Pyotr Tchaikovsky	
Performer	Slovak Philharmonic Orchestra/Halász	
Time	1'13"	
Source	Naxos	

In *The Nutcracker* ballet story the Prince escorts Clara to the Land of Sweets where the Sugar Plum Fairy greets them. The Prince tells her about their daring battle with the army of mice and she rewards them with a celebration that includes this Chinese Dance.

MUSETTE	UNIT 21	TRACK 102
Composer	Johann Sebastian Bach	
Performer	Janos Sebestyen	
Time	0'48"	
Source	Naxos	

Bach's keyboard piece recalls the Musette de cour, a member of the bagpipe family. A feature of all bagpipes is the drone or drones, a note that plays a lower pitch continuously, acting like a bass platform for the melody.

SNOW IN KALAMAZOO	UNIT 22	TRACK 103
Composer	Koos Terpstra	
Performer	Valebjorg, Vettefors, Neuendorf	
Time	3'06"	
Source	Naxos	

Koos Terpstra is a Dutch composer who wrote this piece for three percussion players as a result of a visit to the USA in 1978. The instruments used include marimba, congas, woodblocks and small gong. Kalamazoo lies in the State of Michigan.

FINALE [THE DARGASON]	REVISION UNIT B	TRACK 104
Composer	Gustav Holst	
Performer	Bournemouth Sinfonietta/Studt	
Time	3'24"	
Source	Naxos	

Holst has taken an English dance tune of the 16th century from the *Playford's Dancing Master* [1651] collection. Cleverly, Holst weaves into the proceedings the 16th century song, *Greensleeves*. The name 'Dargason' may have its roots in an Anglo-Saxon word, meaning dwarf or fairy.

Published by The Voices Foundation and Alfred Publishing Co

Key Words

Published by The Voices Foundation and Alfred Publishing Co
© The Voices Foundation 2014

Published by The Voices Foundation and Alfred Publishing Co

Dynamic[s]

A term used in music for the volume of sound.

Handsigns

Handsigns are hand-formed shapes that correlate with the Singing Names. Both are used simultaneously. Each Singing Name has its own specific handsign shape, so that with constant use, the physical memory of the hand shape can prompt the aural memory with the correct pitch.

The handsigns shown here are used for the so-called diatonic notes. The green handsigns are those used in *First Steps: Age 7-11*.

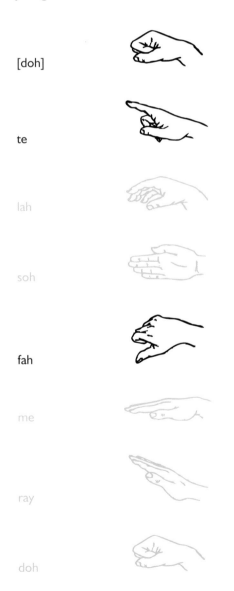

[doh]

te

lah

soh

fah

me

ray

doh

Metre

Rhythm gives rise to the feeling of pulse [heartbeat], and both together set up a sense of 'stronger' and 'less strong' beats. When performed, a piece of music will give rise to a recurring and identifiable pattern of 'strong' and 'weak' beats. For instance, a pattern of: *strong-weak-weak-weak / strong-weak-weak-weak* produces a metre of 4. In music notation the metre is shown as a Time Signature.

Phrase

Phrase is a portion of a melody, consisting of a group of notes that give the impression of 'belonging together'. Singers draw breath before the first note of a phrase and use that to sing the complete phrase. Many melodies notated in this book are shown with phrase marks.

Pitch

This is the melodic aspect of sound. For example, a high sounding melodic note is high in pitch; a low sounding melodic note is low in pitch.

Pitch Interval

This is the pitch-distance between two notes. Two notes of the same pitch are said to be in Unison. The distance between two notes of different pitch can be measured and named: soh and lah are notes of 'next-door-pitch', musically known as a major 2nd; soh and me are notes of a 'jump apart', and make an interval musically known as a minor 3rd.

Pulse

Pulse and beat are usually interchangeable terms.

When patterns of rhythm are performed, a regular sensation of pulse can be felt.

For the purposes of *First Steps: Age 7-11*, pulse is treated as being the 'live' sensation of the music, the heartbeat, so to speak. When performing a song or listening to music, this heartbeat may be shown through movement of parts of the body or simply feeling the sensation with no motion at all.

The word 'beat' on its own can be useful for describing what has been or will be experienced when singing a song. So, for example, 'phrase 1 is eight beats long and phrase 2 is four beats long.'

Published by The Voices Foundation and Alfred Publishing Co
© The Voices Foundation 2014

Rhythm
[NC England: duration]

Rhythm is the 'river' of music. It flows from beginning to end on a continuous tide of sound and sometimes silence. The pattern of longer and shorter sounds in songs largely mimics the pattern of the words in the text, poem or rhyme.

Rhythm Proper Names

These are the names given to identify different rhythm elements. In this book the following are used and identified by their English system name and, in brackets, the American system name. From the note of longest duration: minim [half note]; crotchet [quarter note]; quaver [eighth note]. The names apply to the 'sounding' note and its equivalent 'silence' length, the *rest*.

Rhythm Speaking Names

These are names that help children to develop skills and understanding about rhythm. For example, 'ta' and 'teh-teh' are spoken for two specific elements of rhythm, the crotchet note [quarter note] and two quaver notes [eighth notes]. The names can be used in purely aural work when we wish to identify and perform the elements of a rhythm phrase. They can also be used to identify and perform the rhythm symbols when reading or writing music notation. A speaking name is a useful device for assimilating and securing a new rhythm element. Once the rhythm element is secured in notation, then the speaking name will gradually become redundant.

Rhythm Sol-fa

This is a form of melodic notation. It results from combining rhythm symbols and singing name letters, eg d [doh]; r [ray]. The notation appears in a horizontal format and does not use the stave [staff].

Singing Names [Sol-fa]

These are the names of melodic notes that singers can find very helpful. They are more usually known by the collective name of sol-fa. The names, for example, soh [s], me [m], lah [l], used in conjunction with their handsigns, can be used by singers to understand the relationship between sounds of different pitch, and over a period of time assist them in developing a useful music reading ability.

Structure

A melody is normally built of several phrases. Usually there is an element of melodic repetition and difference between the phrases. Labelling the phrases with uppercase letters can identify the repetition and difference. The first phrase is labelled A. If the next phrase is a repetition, then it too is labelled A. If it is musically different, then it is labelled B. A third different phrase will be labelled C, and so on. Repetition plays a large part in the structure of music, so typically a four-phrase song could musically be A B B A.

Tempo

This is the rate of pace at which the pulse moves.

Texture

Texture is word used to describe the musical density of a piece of music. It can be likened to the weave in a fabric. So, an unaccompanied melody is a single 'weave' of rhythm and pitch, whereas music for two voices or instrumental parts is like a double 'weave'.

Timbre

This word is used when speaking of the tone-colour or characteristic quality of sound. Timbre enables the ear to distinguish the difference between, say, a child, woman and man singing the same song.

Tone-set

A melody will use a series of pitch sounds and most, if not all, will be used more than once. When these pitches are collated, using their sol-fa initial letters, they form a tone-set, eg l-s-m-d. The tone-set is always shown with the highest pitch first and the others in descending order.

Published by The Voices Foundation and Alfred Publishing Co

Song Melodies

Published by The Voices Foundation and Alfred Publishing Co
© The Voices Foundation 2014

Read In Rhythm

These melodies are drawn from the programme's song repertoire. All the rhythm and pitch elements form part of the concept teaching and learning in **First Steps**.

This section is principally designed to give teachers themselves further opportunities to become familiar with reading rhythm sol-fa notation.

The examples might be used with children at the appropriate points in the teaching as further practice for their reading, mostly in the latter part of the course.

Published by The Voices Foundation and Alfred Publishing Co

Tone-set Index

Published by The Voices Foundation and Alfred Publishing Co
© The Voices Foundation 2014

Song Melodies to read in rhythm sol-fa notation

Ev'ryone, good morning

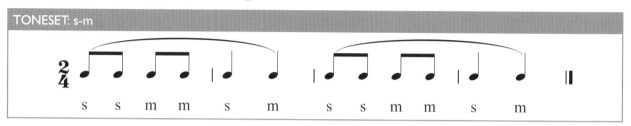

Fire! Fire!

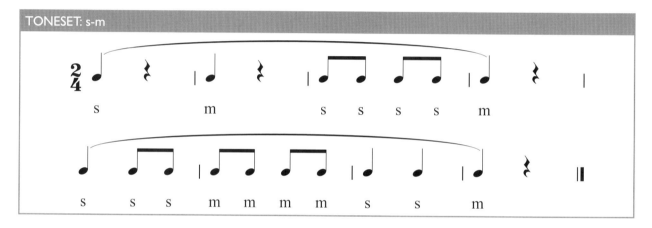

Here I come

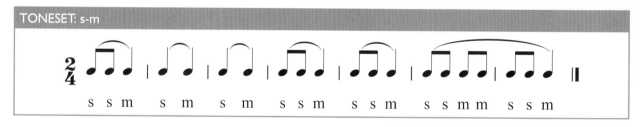

I like coffee, I like tea

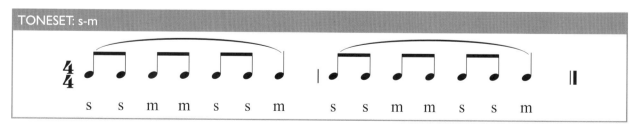

Published by The Voices Foundation and Alfred Publishing Co

I, I, me oh my

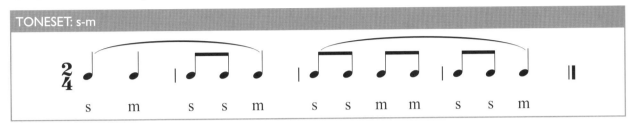

Apple tree

Bounce high, bounce low

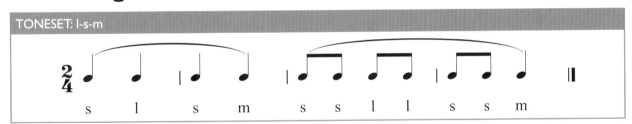

Doggie, doggie

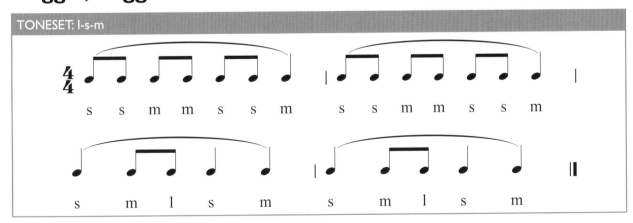

Published by The Voices Foundation and Alfred Publishing Co
© The Voices Foundation 2014

Here sits a fat cat

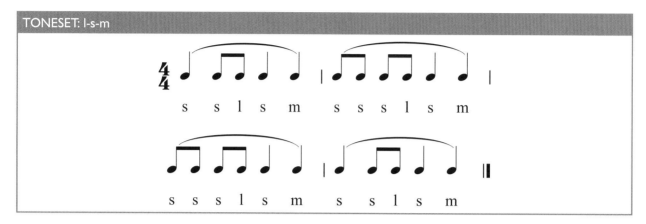

TONESET: l-s-m

John the blacksmith

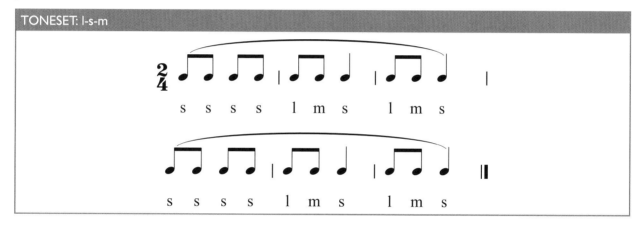

TONESET: l-s-m

Plainie clappie

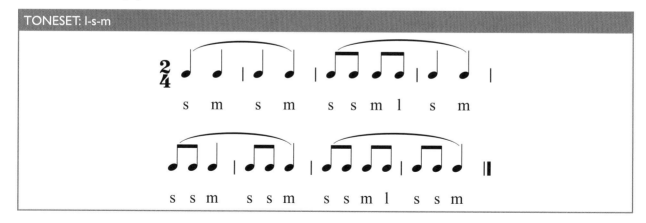

TONESET: l-s-m

Published by The Voices Foundation and Alfred Publishing Co

Rain, rain, go away

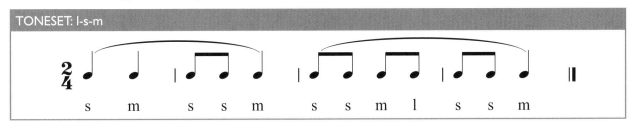

Row, boat, row

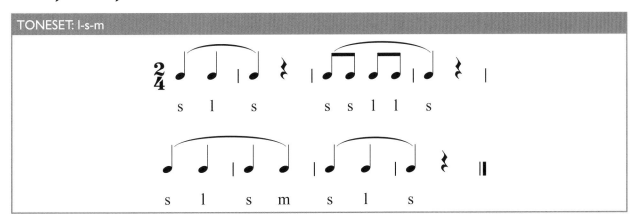

Rain on the green grass

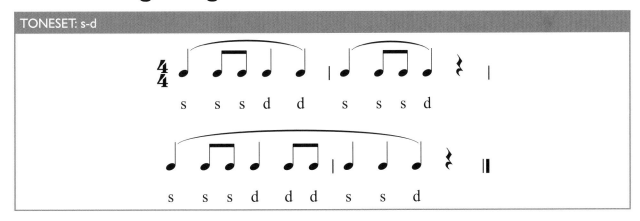

Published by The Voices Foundation and Alfred Publishing Co
© The Voices Foundation 2014

Can you tap this rhythm?

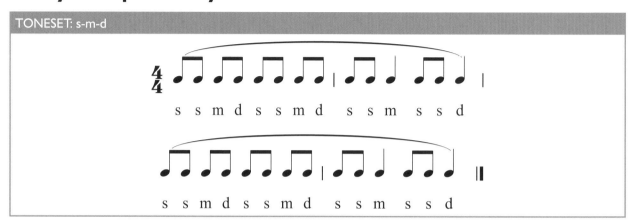

Spinning top

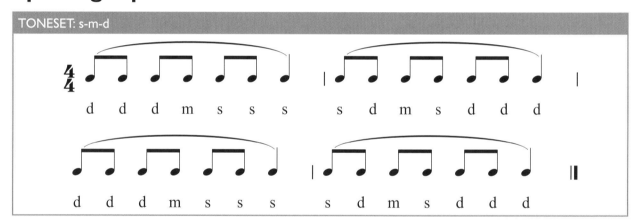

I have lost the cupboard key

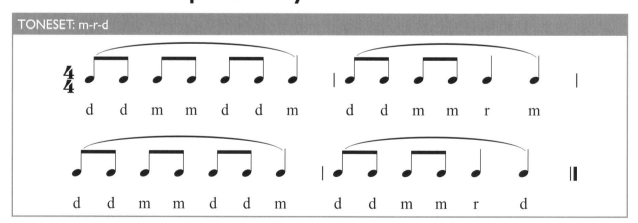

Published by The Voices Foundation and Alfred Publishing Co
© The Voices Foundation 2014

One for the mouse

TONESET: m-r-d

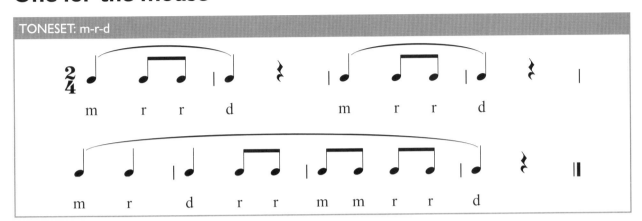

Rain is falling down

TONESET: m-r-d

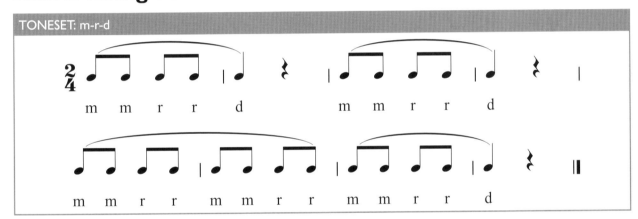

Suo gân

TONESET: m-r-d

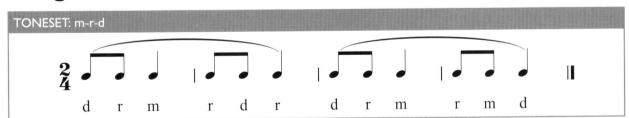

Published by The Voices Foundation and Alfred Publishing Co
© The Voices Foundation 2014

Lots of rosy apples

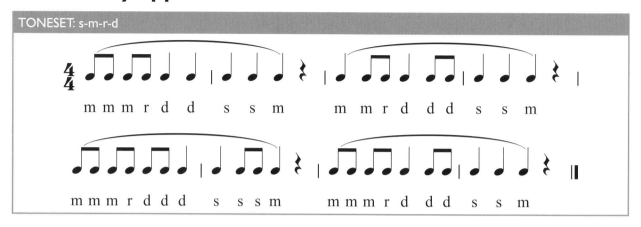

Bow wow wow

Button you must wander

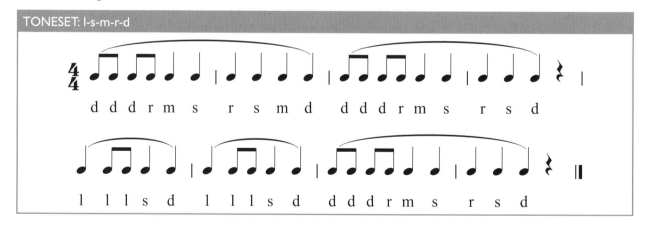

Chest, chest, knee, toe

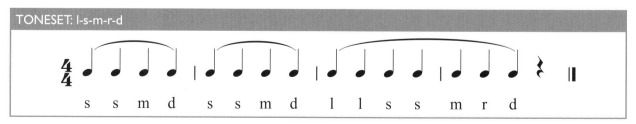

Published by The Voices Foundation and Alfred Publishing Co
© The Voices Foundation 2014

Coca-Cola went to town

TONESET: l-s-m-r-d

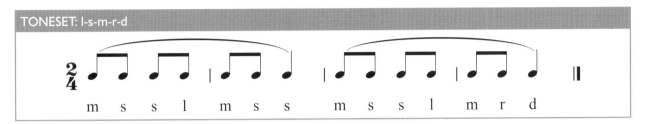

m s s l m s s m s s l m r d

Engine, engine

TONESET: l-s-m-r-d

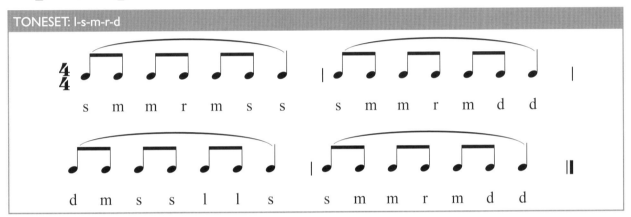

s m m r m s s s m m r m d d

d m s s l l s s m m r m d d

Rocky mountain

TONESET: l-s-m-r-d

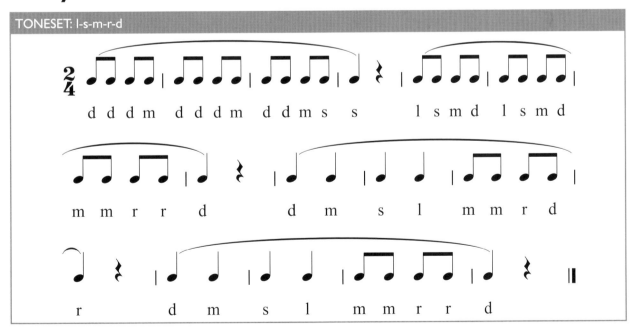

d d d m d d d m d d m s s l s m d l s m d

m m r r d d m s l m m r d

r d m s l m m r r d

Published by The Voices Foundation and Alfred Publishing Co
© The Voices Foundation 2014

Salani

TONESET: l-s-m-r-d

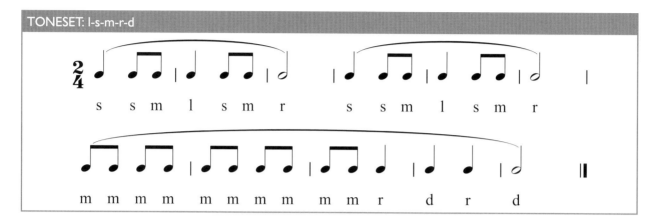

Starlight, star bright

TONESET: l-s-m-r-d

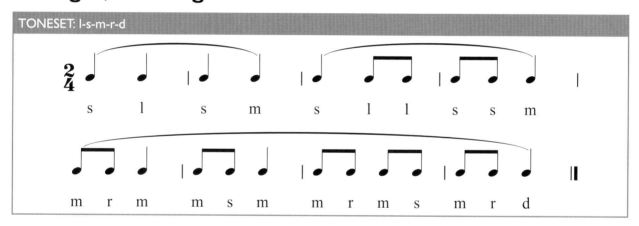

Published by The Voices Foundation and Alfred Publishing Co
© The Voices Foundation 2014

The CDs

Published by The Voices Foundation and Alfred Publishing Co
© The Voices Foundation 2014

Song Index

Published by The Voices Foundation and Alfred Publishing Co
© The Voices Foundation 2014

COMPOSER	TITLE	CD-2 TRACK
Bach	Badinerie	70
Daquin	Le Coucou	71
Ibert	Parade	72
Hertel/Lanchbery	Clog Dance	73
Prokofiev	The Bird, The Duck, The Cat	74, 75, 76
Saint-Saëns	The Swan	77
Kodály	The Viennese Musical Clock	78
Tchaikovsky	March	79
Traditional Russian	Where are you?	80
Grieg	In the Hall of the Mountain King	81
Britten	Percussion	82
Hildegard	O Euchari	83
Shatin	Nun, Gimel, Hei, Shin	84
Britten	Oliver Cromwell	85
Handel	The Arrival of the Queen of Sheba	86
Pitfield	Toccata	87
Villa-Lobos	O Polichinelo	88
Villa-Lobos	A Pobrezinha	89
Mussorgsky	Bydło	90
Rimsky-Korsakov	Flight of the Bumblebee	91
Anonymous	The Green Man	92
Traditional Tibet	Sangva Duva	93
Tchaikovsky	Arabian Dance	94
Anderson	The Typewriter	95
Anonymous	Under the Greenwood Tree	96
Hildegard	O Pastor Animarum	97
Warlock	Pavane	98
Hampton	Tempo's Boogie	99
Holst	Ostinato	100
Tchaikovsky	Chinese Dance	101
Bach	Musette	102
Terpstra	Snow in Kalamazoo	103
Holst	The Dargason	104

Published by The Voices Foundation and Alfred Publishing Co
© The Voices Foundation 2014

Files On CD-2

Unit Display Examples

From Unit 15 onwards there are a number of Teaching Ideas that ask the teacher to display a music example for the class to see and read. When an example is needed, the graphic could be projected directly from the CD and computer or downloaded and printed.

The Rhythm Cards

These provide reading material for the children. They can be downloaded and printed as laminated cards or projected on to a white board. The Units will indicate to the teacher when they could be used for teaching purposes.

Teaching Record

This sheet contains the Teaching Sequence to be found on pages 24-27. In addition it will enable the teacher to keep a record of the Units completed and allows space for comment.

Planning Template

When printed, this sheet gives the teacher a Unit planning tool. It can also be found on page 13 in the handbook.

Published by The Voices Foundation and Alfred Publishing Co
© The Voices Foundation 2014